The Jazz Ensemble
A GUIDE TO TECHNIQUE

Robert E. Henry

A SPECTRUM BOOK

PRENTICE-HALL, INC., Englewood Cliffs, New Jersey 07632

Library of Congress Cataloging in Publication Data

HENRY, ROBERT E
    The jazz ensemble.

    (A Spectrum Book)
    Bibliographies: p.
    1. Jazz music—Instruction and study. 2. Jazz
ensembles—Instruction and study. 3. Big band music—
Instruction and study. I. Title.
MT86.H47   785.42   80-23360
    ISBN 0-13-509992-7
    ISBN 0-13-509984-6 (pbk.)

To my father, Hiram H. Henry, who was and still is my greatest professional and personal inspiration.

Editorial/production supervision and interior design by
    Louise M. Marcewicz
Cover design by Judith Kazdym Leeds
Manufacturing buyer: Barbara A. Frick

PRENTICE-HALL INTERNATIONAL, INC., *London*
PRENTICE-HALL OF AUSTRALIA PTY. LIMITED, *Sydney*
PRENTICE-HALL OF CANADA, LTD., *Toronto*
PRENTICE-HALL OF INDIA PRIVATE LIMITED, *New Delhi*
PRENTICE-HALL OF JAPAN, INC., *Tokyo*
PRENTICE-HALL OF SOUTHEAST ASIA PTE. LTD., *Singapore*
WHITEHALL BOOKS LIMITED, *Wellington, New Zealand*

Contents

Foreword

The rise of jazz education in this country has been one of the most significant, if relatively unheralded, events in our cultural history. As a creative art form born in America, jazz has existed for about a century, dating from around the late 1880's, when Buddy Bolden established himself as the legendary (though unrecorded) progenitor of jazz. It took thirty years for the general public to begin to accept jazz as a valid form of music, to write articles about it, and to capture some of the performances on records. Even so, controversies about its legitimacy as a music form raged on, even to the present day in a diminishing number of circles. It was another thirty years before jazz was studied in a university—North Texas State University in the late 1940's. By this time, sixty years after Buddy Bolden, jazz was internationally recognized and imitated and was frequently referred to as "America's only original art form."

The shift to study in a university setting after World War II was an important one. Though major jazz performers were in abundance for many decades prior to the first university course, little had been done to analyze or develop a methodology for these performers. The performers themselves, furthermore, exhibited little interest in teaching jazz. This was a dangerous situation since it might have led to having the music researched and taught by jazz-loving pedagogues who were not creditable performers themselves, which would affect their course syllabi, their books and methods, their in-class demonstrations, and their ability to remain abreast of current practices in the professional circles of jazz. Though this pitfall wasn't avoided altogether, a sufficient number of highly regarded, practicing professionals turned their attention to pioneering jazz education. Prior to the 1960's, very few books were written on jazz other than fanciful efforts at books on the history of jazz, mostly written by nonperforming authors who generally focused their attention on prehistoric influences, biographical sketches, anecdotal material, and the sociological aspects of jazz. The only books published before 1960 that proved to be valuable to the aspiring young jazz musician were Russ Garcia's *Professional Arranger-Composer,* George Russell's *Lydian Concept,* and John Mehegan's *Jazz Improvisation,* all written in the 1950's. But in the two decades that followed, many fine books emerged that covered most of the needed areas of jazz study that were being taken up in the universities, including improvisation, arranging, history/appreciation, analysis of jazz styles, ear-training, pedagogy, and prerecorded accompaniment.

The pioneers of university degree programs in jazz were North Texas State University, Westlake College of Music, and Berklee School of Music. But the jazz curriculum has been sculpted to near perfection, after years of experimentation and review, at places such as University of Miami, Indiana University, University of Utah, and Arizona State University. At this time, nearly a hundred years after Buddy Bolden, the university jazz programs have finally been developed to the point where the course offerings reflect professional practices, and a time when the graduating students of the jazz programs are generally very successful in the professional field.

Now that the jazz curriculum has become a highly-developed course of study, we can, for the first time, make an accurate assessment of which specific topics have yet to be organized into a corresponding method and/or book. (During the early days of jazz education, we frequently found ourselves teaching a new jazz course for which there was no usable text.) The topical content of jazz programs will vary from one institution to another, especially with regard to the inclusion of courses such as analysis of jazz styles, ear-training, jazz piano for non-pianists, pedagogy, tune study, rhythm section classes, and recitals, but the "core courses" of jazz, namely jazz ensemble, improvisation, arranging, and jazz history, are generally included in all programs (even those which do not lead to a degree in jazz). Of those core courses, it is strange to find that adequate materials have been published in all but the most common course of all . . .*the jazz ensemble,* which is always the first (and sometimes the only) course in a new jazz program. Whether or not we agree and/or approve, most jazz programs are evaluated by potential students, the university, and other schools, on the strength of their jazz ensemble.

To be accurate, there *have* been books, even good ones, on the jazz ensemble, but there has never been one of the scope and magnitude of this one by Robert Henry. It is complete enough to be used in jazz pedagogy classes, which this writer intends to do. It also serves the jazz ensemble director who is already in service, but senses a need for a more complete understanding of the subject. Best of all, perhaps, even the *members* of jazz ensembles can obtain great benefit from reading and applying the principles contained herein. Because I have adjudicated many high school and college festivals over the last twenty years, the reading of Mr. Henry's book was, for me, like reading a well-organized compilation of all the problems (and their *solutions*) experienced by the bands, their directors, and the adjudicators themselves.

Particularly impressive is the manner in which Robert Henry approaches each problem of the jazz ensemble. Each topic is defined, described, and illustrated by numerous original examples, excerpted passages from published arrangements, and even diagrams which describe nonverbal mental concepts. This is followed by procedural methods which include matters of organization and sequence as well as special aids: tuning charts, useful terminology with which to communicate phrasing concepts to the ensemble, phrasing practices of specific rhythmic-melodic clichés found in many jazz arrangements, scat-singing phonetics that accurately describe proper phrasing, and differing interpretations due to specific sub-styles within jazz such as swing, bebop, rock, and bossa nova). To round out the discussion of each topic, he lists specific problems which may occur even when his system is being applied! For example, after describing tuning procedures in great detail, the author has the insight to list "Specific Problems in Intonation," which describes problems that may surface because of the nature of the arrangement, such as unison passages, crescendos and diminuendos, accented passages, pedal tones in trombones, and so on.

Professor Henry is aware of all the books on jazz and is quick to make specific recommendations to the reader, especially when it pertains to the topic under discussion at the time. Bibliography is an important part of each chapter and appendix in the book. It is indeed refreshing to read a book on jazz that offers means of continuing investigation to the reader by listing important books other than his own. All too often, an author will expect the reader to believe that his book is unique and unparalleled, depriving students of further investigation by not leading them to other helpful sources. Appendix B also lists names and addresses of all the major publishers of arrangements, an invaluable aid to anyone connected with jazz ensembles.

Perhaps the most important segments of the book, because they answer so many questions and problems of the typical jazz ensemble, are the sections on music selection and programming, planning and conducting rehearsals, improvisation, and the rhythm section. Careful understanding, assimilation, and application of the concepts and principles contained in these sections would greatly improve the performance of any jazz ensemble. I sincerely believe that this book by Robert Henry will become the standard text on jazz ensembles in the near future.

Jerry Coker
Big Creek Music Seminary
Marshall, North Carolina

Preface

This book is meant for readers who have a basic understanding of music and musical terms. The text can be used as a guide toward an understanding of jazz styles and performance techniques as well as pedagogical applications.

Throughout, references are made to more detailed works on specific subject areas for further, more in-depth study. Additionally, appendices are provided to help the reader in obtaining even more knowledge and materials for study.

Acknowledgments

I would like to make special thanks to several people whose gracious help greatly facilitated the writing of this book.

Janie, Donna, and Terri for proofreading the rough manuscript and giving editorial suggestions.

The many students who participated throughout the development of this manuscript in my jazz techniques and jazz ensemble classes.

Dr. Donald McGlothlin, Chairman of the Department of Music at the University of Missouri-Columbia, who has encouraged the development of the jazz program at UMC and who is constantly searching for new and different approaches to upgrade the entirety of music.

The Ensemble 1

This chapter addresses itself to the generalized areas concerning jazz ensemble playing as a whole. The four subsequent chapters delve into more specific areas of jazz performance.

Of course, everyone strives to achieve the best sound possible with any type of performance group whether it be jazz ensemble, concert band, orchestra, choir, or otherwise. In each of these situations, every individual musician must blend and match his sound (tuning, tone, volume, projection, vibrato, etc.) both with the ensemble and within his section.

One of the most important factors determining the sound of an ensemble is whether or not the ensemble plays in tune. Time should be spent tuning any ensemble before each performance and rehearsal. Every director probably has his or her own unique way of tuning the ensemble, each spending a different amount of time. Because of the size of the typical jazz ensemble, little time is needed to tune each individual instrument. The simplest and easiest way to tune every instrument is with a strobotuner or some similar electronic device.

TUNING AND INTONATION

Although the use of an electronic tuning device may be the simplest and easiest means, it cannot substitute for careful listening on the part of the players. Intonation will change according to range, dynamic level, etc., making it necessary to constantly adjust the tuning throughout.

The fixed pitch instruments such as the acoustic piano (since it would be rather awkward to tune for every rehearsal), most electric pianos (some have easily accessible tuning adjustment controls), vibes, marimbas, and so forth are the basis for the tuning pitch of the ensemble.

Following are a few simple methods of tuning and listening to intonation without the use of an electronic tuning device.

Tune the lead trumpet or alto to the piano or other fixed pitch instrument, concert pitch "A" or "B-flat," the trumpet being preferred.

Next, the lead trumpet (or lead alto) tunes each section's lead player, the alto to "A" or "B-flat," and the trombone to "B-flat." It is sometimes better to tune the lead trombone to the piano "B-flat" an octave lower than the trumpet's concert "B-flat."

Next, the lead player of each section tunes the other players in the section in one of three ways:

The "Match" System   The lead player plays the tuning note for four beats and stops. Then the next player plays four beats and stops, striving for a match in pitch and tone. This is continued throughout the section. (Fig. 1-1A)

Figure 1–1a

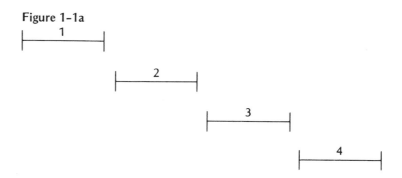

A variation of this system is to have the lead player play the tuning note between each of the different players' tuning notes. This variation is more effective for less experienced members of the group. (Fig. 1-1B)

Figure 1–1b

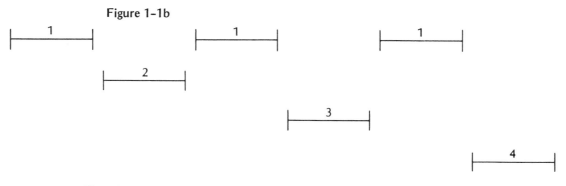

The "Sustain" System   The lead player sustains the tuning note while the other section players enter at different measured intervals, for two or four beats, and sustain the note until everyone in the section is playing the note together. This will quickly reveal an out-of-tune player at the point of entry. (Fig.1-2)

Figure 1-2

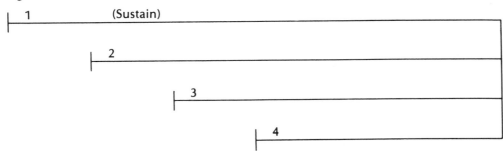

The "Intervallic" System   The lead player tunes using intervals of a third, fourth, fifth, and sixth in addition to the unison and octave. To first tune the unison or octave with the piano, the lead player will sustain the tuning concert pitch "A" or "B-flat" while the piano plays the concert pitch "A" or "B-flat" in octaves. The piano player will then release this, striking the octave again adding the fifth, release, then proceed to play a simple chord progression under the sustaining player. (Fig. 1-3A)

Figure 1-3a

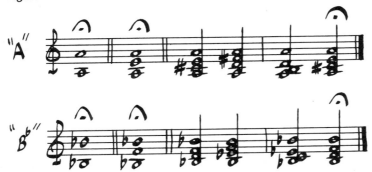

Next, the lead player tunes using intervals while the piano is sustaining the single (or octave) tuning pitch "A" or "B-flat". (Fig. 1-3B)

Figure 1-3b

This intervallic system can be used throughout a section using various players to sustain the tuning pitch while others play the intervals.

Another method of listening to tuning and intonation for the entire ensemble is an adaptation of a simple series of exercises. They were developed and used by Hiram H. Henry with his concert bands at Oklahoma State University. (Fig. 1-4)

Figure 1–4a   Key Chart

C		C	F	B♭	E♭	A♭	D♭	G♭–F♯	B	E	A	D	G
E♭		A	D	G	C	F	B♭	E♭–D♯	G♯	C♯	F♯	B	E
B♭		D	G	C	F	B♭	E♭	A♭–G♯	C♯	F♯	B	E	A
𝄢		C	F	B♭	E♭	A♭	D♭	G♭–F♯	B	E	A	D	G

Sequence

1. *Play Scales*   Use major, minor, and modal scales changing keys often. An excellent book containing many scales is *Scales for Jazz Improvisation* by Dan Haerle.[1] Run the scales in patterns at times. Another excellent book contains these scale patterns, *Patterns for Jazz* by Jerry Coker et al.[2]

2. *Play arpeggios*   Use major and minor triads, and seventh chords. This is sometimes called "chord-running."

Figure 1–4b

1 3 5 8   5 3 1   1 3 5 ♭7   5 3 1

(Change keys often.)

3. *Play arpeggios stopping on an assigned chord tone*   Then sustain until all chord tones are heard simultaneously. Change keys often. Vary the pitches that each part sustains from time to time.

[1]Lebanon, IN: Studio P/R, Inc., 1975.
[2]Lebanon, IN: Studio P/R, Inc., 1970.

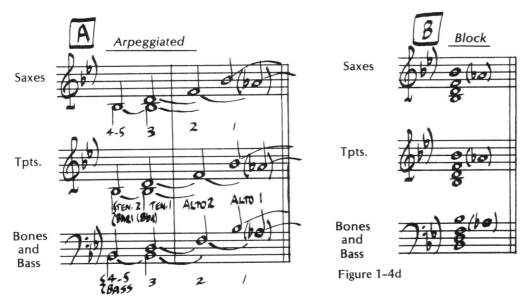

Figure 1–4c

Figure 1–4d

C Figure 1–4e.   Moving Block (Play chord tones: left to right.)

Alto 1, Tpt. 1, Bone 1	8 ($\flat$7)	1	3	5	8 ($\flat$7)
Alto 2, Tpt. 2, Bone 2	5	8 ($\flat$7)	1	3	5
Tenor 1, Tpt. 3, Bone 3	3	5	8 ($\flat$7)	1	3
Tenor 2, Bari, Tpt. 4–5, Bone 4–5	1	3	5	8 ($\flat$7)	1

   4.   *Play chord patterns*   (Change keys often.)

Figure 1–4f

The Ensemble   **5**

Figure 1–4g

Figure 1–4h

Figure 1–4i

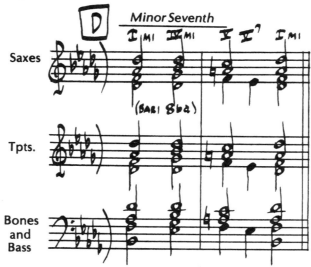

5. *Play octave tuning exercise*

Figure 1–4j

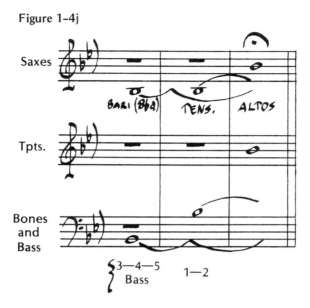

Equally important to tuning the wind instruments is proper tuning of the rhythm section.

The variable pitch instruments of the rhythm section are the bass and guitar. Following are the tuning pitches for the bass and guitar (Fig. 1-5):

There are four basic methods of tuning the variable-pitch instruments.

One way to tune a variable-pitch instrument is with an electronic strobe device that has been adjusted to match the tuning of a fixed-pitch instrument. The variable-pitch instruments can play each string in front of the microphone and observe when the pitch comes in tune by turning the tuning gears. If the instruments are electric, they can be plugged directly into the microphone input jack.

Another method is to take each note from the piano. (See Fig. 1-5.)

A better method for fretted instruments is to take the low "E" note from the piano and tune the other strings to each other by the following method (Fig. 1-6):

1. Play the 5th fret "A" on the low E-string and tune the open A-string to that pitch.

2. Play the 5th fret "D" on the A-string and tune the open D-string to that pitch.

3. Play the 5th fret "G" on the D-string and tune the open G-string to that pitch.

4. Play the 4th fret "B" on the G-string and tune the open B-string to that pitch.

5. Play the 5th fret "E" on the B-string and tune the high E-string to that pitch.

GUITAR

BASS

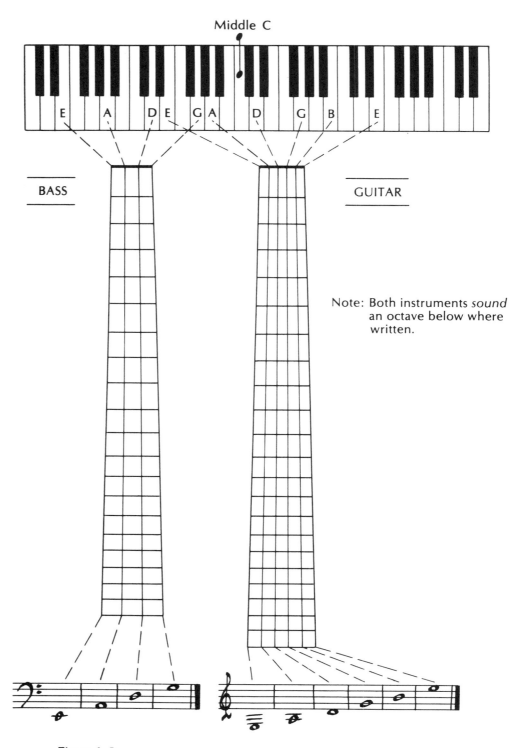

Note: Both instruments *sound*
an octave below where
written.

Figure 1-5

The best method of tuning and listening to intonation is through use of
harmonics. Harmonics, simply stated, are overtones of the strings. Strings
can vibrate as a whole, in halves, thirds, fourths, fifths, and so on. These
overtones can be isolated for tuning purposes by very lightly touching a

string at certain points. Kent Wheeler Kennan describes these in his book *The Technique of Orchestration*.[3]

Figure 1–6

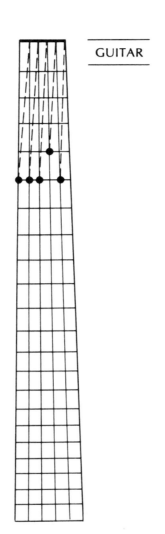

BASS

GUITAR

a. In the middle (an octave above the pitch of the open string); the result is a harmonic an octave higher than the pitch of the open string. [On a fretted instrument, this would occur at the 12th fret.]

b. One third of the string length from either end (either a perfect 5th above the open pitch or at the point where the note would ordinarily be played); the result is a harmonic an octave and a 5th higher than the open pitch. [On a fretted instrument, this would occur at the 7th or 19th fret.]

c. One fourth of the string length from either end (either a perfect 4th above the open pitch or at the point where the note would ordinarily be played); the result is a harmonic two

[3]Kent Wheeler Kennan, *The Technique of Orchestration*, 2nd ed. (Englewood Cliffs, NJ: Prentice-Hall, Inc., ©1970), pp. 67-68.

octaves higher than the open pitch. [On a fretted instrument, this would occur at the 5th fret.]

d.   One fifth of the string length from either end (either a major 3rd above the open pitch or at the point where the note would ordinarily be played) or two fifths of the string length from either end (either a major 6th or a major 10th above the open pitch); the result is a harmonic two octaves and a major 3rd higher than the open pitch. [On a fretted instrument, this would occur at the 4th, 9th, and 16th frets.]

The application of these harmonics to tuning results in a much finer degree of ability to match pitches. When tuning two harmonics together, you must get the two harmonics to create one pitch that is straight and that contains no "beats" or "pulsations" which result when the notes are out of tune. The faster the pulsation, the more out of tune they are. The slower the pulsations, the closer the notes are to being in tune. It is much easier to detect these pulsations when using harmonics.

Figure 1–7

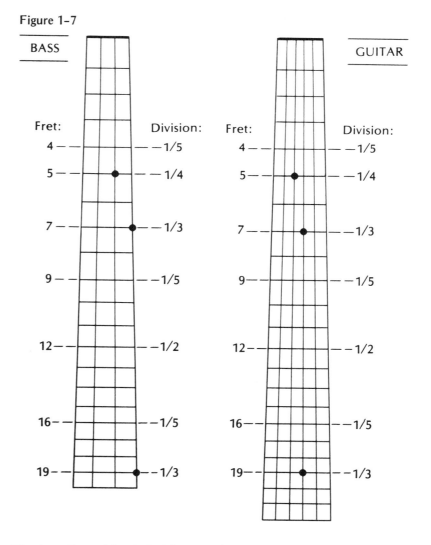

Use the following harmonics procedure to tune the bass or guitar:

1.   Tune the open G-string to the piano.

2.   Lightly touch the G-string at the one-third point from either end (7th or 19th fret) to produce the harmonic of an octave and a fifth above the open string. This should sustain sufficient time to allow you to lightly touch the D-string at the one-fourth point (5th fret) to produce the harmonic two octaves above that open string. These two harmonics should match without any pulsations when in tune. (Fig. 1-7)

3.   Tune the A-string to the D-string by the same method. Play the harmonic on the D-string produced by the one-third division (7th or 19th fret) and match the harmonic produced by dividing the A-string into fourths (5th fret). (Fig. 1-8)

Figure 1–8

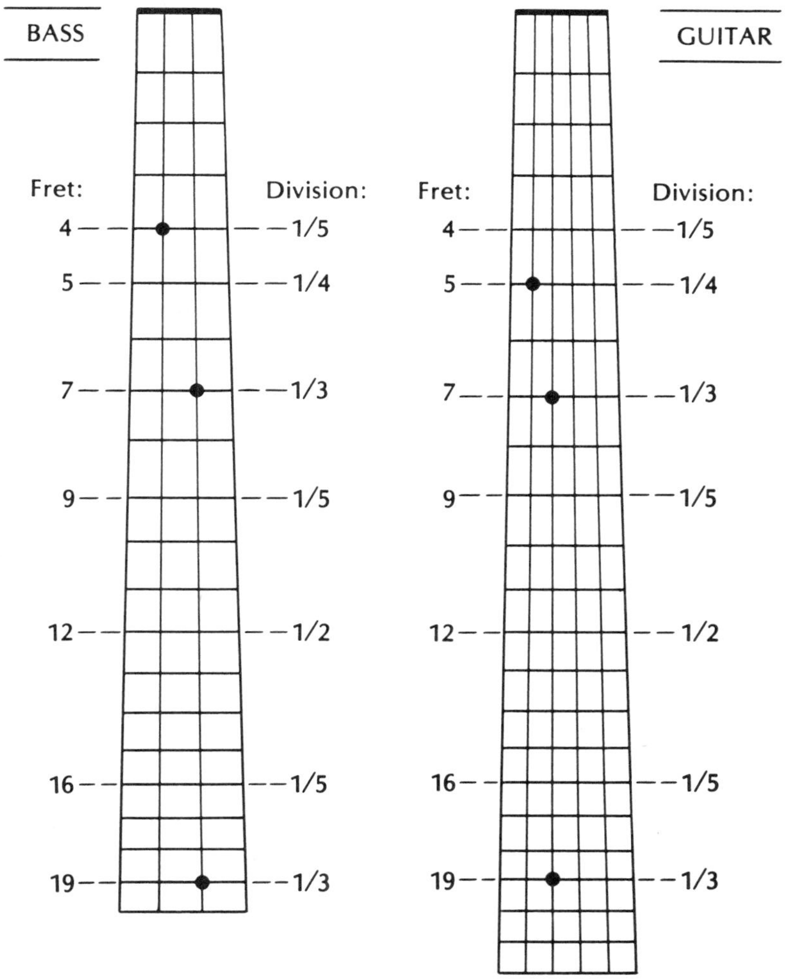

4. Tune the low E-string to the A-string. The one-third (7th or 19th fret) A-string harmonic equals the one-fourth (5th fret) low E-string harmonic. (Fig. 1-9)

Figure 1–9

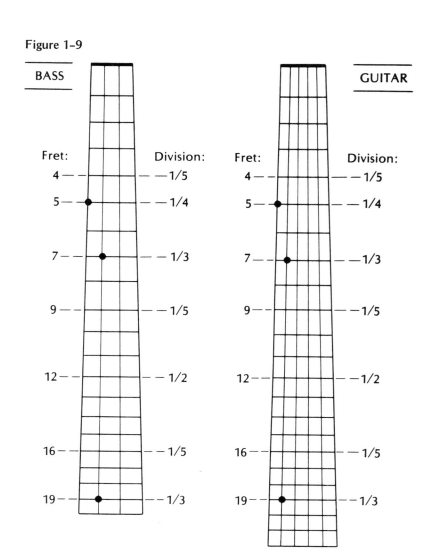

For guitarists, two more strings must be dealt with: To tune the B-string, several approaches may be taken. One is to play the one-third (7th or 19th fret) harmonic on the low E-string which is the same pitch as the open B-string. Another way is to play the harmonic on the G-string produced by dividing the string into fifths (4th, 9th, or 16th frets) and match the harmonic on the B-string produced by dividing the string into fourths (5th fret). (Fig. 1-10)

The high E-string can likewise be tuned several ways. One way is to divide the low E-string into fourths (5th fret), which produces the same pitch of the open high E-string. Another is to take the one-third (7th or 19th fret) harmonic of the A-string, which also produces the same pitch as the open high E-string. (Fig. 1-11)

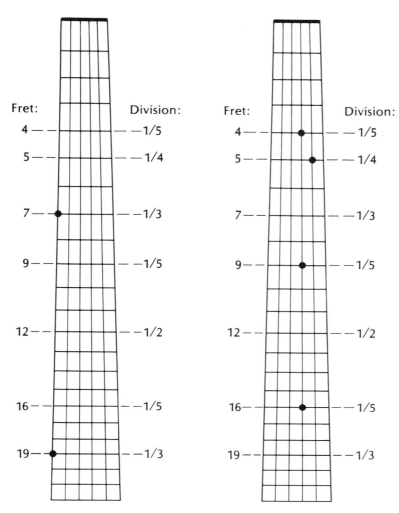

Fret: Division:
4 — — — — 1/5
5 — — — — 1/4
7 — ● — — 1/3
9 — — — — 1/5
12 — — — — 1/2
16 — — — — 1/5
19 — ● — — 1/3

Fret: Division:
4 — — ● — — 1/5
5 — — ● — — 1/4
7 — — — — 1/3
9 — — ● — — 1/5
12 — — — — 1/2
16 — — ● — — 1/5
19 — — — — 1/3

Figure 1–10

Once the initial tuning has been completed by the entire ensemble, it is beneficial to play through some sort of simple exercise using chordal aspects, such as chorales, stressing the importance of listening to and adjusting each note to be in tune. One jazz method book available that includes tuning and intonation exercises is *Modern Stage Band Techniques* by Dr. M.E. Hall.[4]

Always remember that it is not enough just to get one note in tune. Continual adjustments must be made. Each player must also know the characteristics of his or her own instrument in order to play in tune by being aware of alternate fingerings or positions that will compensate for notes that tend to be out of tune. A tuning chart like the one used at Oklahoma State University could be used to mark notes which are in tune and notes which are commonly out of tune. The chart can then be referred to at regular intervals so that the students may check their progress in learning to adjust problematic notes. (Figs. 1-12A and 1-12B)

[4]San Antonio, TX: Southern Music Company, 1975.

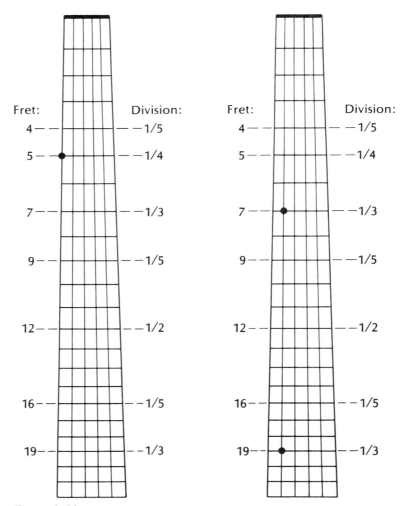

Fret:	Division:		Fret:	Division:
4	1/5		4	1/5
5	1/4		5	1/4
7	1/3		7	1/3
9	1/5		9	1/5
12	1/2		12	1/2
16	1/5		16	1/5
19	1/3		19	1/3

Figure 1–11

Saxophone players tend to go flat in a crescendo (◁‾‾‾) and sharp in a diminuendo (▷‾‾‾). This is probably due to pinching the embouchure or dropping the jaw, combined with increased or decreased air pressure. Brass players tend to go sharp in a crescendo (◁‾‾‾) and flat in a diminuendo (▷‾‾‾) due to an increase or decrease in air pressure without corresponding embouchure compensation.

Some specific problems of intonation occur in the following instances:

1. Unisons, especially in higher registers

2. Open octaves

3. Crescendos and diminuendos

4. Loud passages and accents

5. Soft passages, especially in the brass (There is a tendency to go flat from lack of support.)

6. Pedal tones in the trombones (They tend to be sharp.)

7. Certain combinations of instruments in soli or duet style passages

TUNING CHART—

Name _____

Instrument _____

Markings: Flat   = ♭ or ♭♭
            Sharp   = # or X
            In Tune = ✓

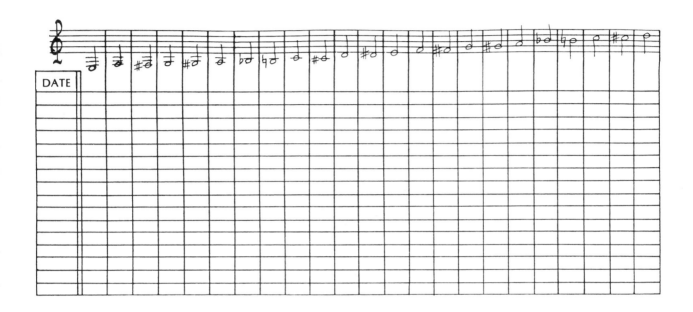

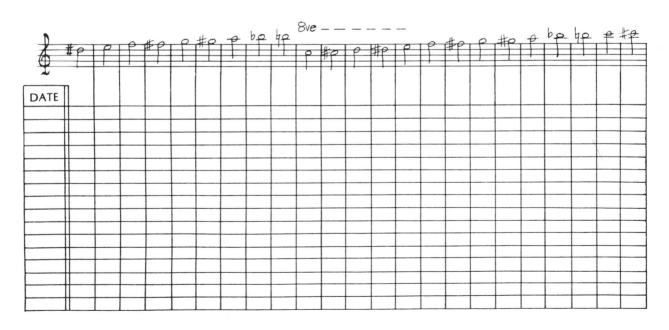

Figure 1–12a

Name _____

Instrument _____

Markings: Flat   = ♭ or ♭♭
          Sharp = # or X
          In Tune = ✓

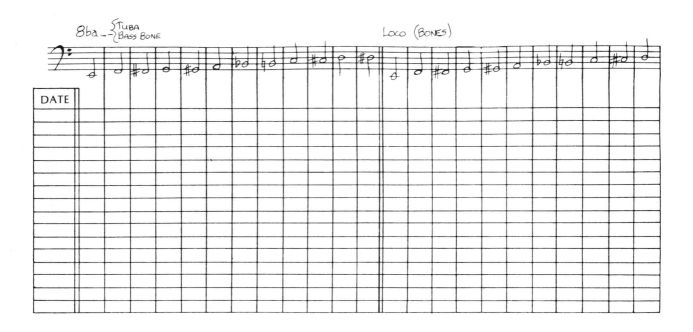

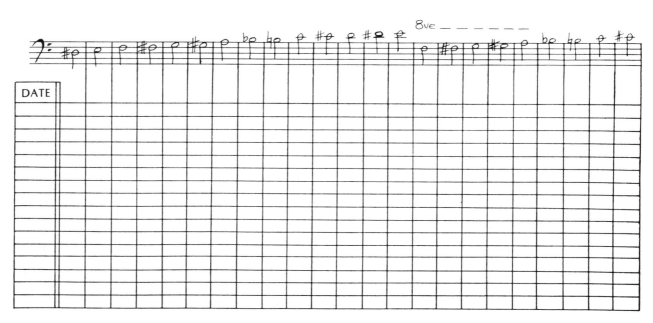

Figure 1–12b

There are three *basic* tones found in ensemble playing, excluding special effects, which will be discussed in Chapter 4.

Straight, full tone   Straight, or full tones, are used in tuning, unison passages, fast-moving runs, and so on.

Moderately fast vibrato   Moderately fast vibratos, whether the passage be slow or fast, are conducive to blending a solo, section, or ensemble in flowing passages.

Moderately slow vibrato   Usually suggested by the character of the tune or the taste of a soloist or director. Moderately slow vibratos are usually found in ballads and slower tunes.

At times, the reeds find it necessary to play with subtones. (Subtones are discussed in Chapter 4.) This effect must be used with discretion and control. In addition, the rhythm section must regulate their sound, volume in particular, so as not to force the horns to overblow and lose the balance of the ensemble.

The balance and blend of an ensemble fall into two basic categories: within a section and within the entire ensemble.

BALANCE AND BLEND

Within a section   Within a section, the lead player's importance must be stressed. All other players must *support* and *enhance* the lead by "playing up to the lead." It is important not to overpower the lead. The volume and tone quality must be blended; and the style, quality, and quantity of vibrato must be matched and patterned after the lead player. Any discrepancies will affect and alter the balance of chordal passages. Sometimes the lead in the sax section will switch, most usually to a tenor as in Jimmy Giuffre's "Four Brothers."[5] In this instance, the sax section must adjust accordingly to follow the style, tone, and volume of the tenor lead. Another variation of sax lead is the octave doubling of the lead by the bari sax player.

Ensemble   Ensemble (tutti) passages use dynamic markings as indicators of volume *only*. Everything is to be played relative to the lead trumpet. As in sectional balance and blend, the lead player (in this instance, the lead trumpet) establishes the volume, tone quality, vibrato, and so on with the ensemble assuming the supportive role. (Fig. 1-13)

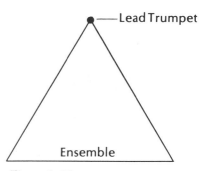

Figure 1-13

Some specific things to watch for in ensemble passages are:

[5] Jimmy Giuffre, Edwin H. Morris and Co., Inc., distributed by Charles Hansen, 1973.

Modulatory passages   The modulating parts, moving notes, need to be clearly heard without overpowering the melody or lead part.

Style interpretation, phrasing, and articulation   These aspects of each passage have to be uniform throughout the band. Differences will result in an unsatisfactory performance. (More in-depth discussions of these areas are found in subsequent chapters.)

Tone quality   Be sure to match tone throughout the entire band. A poor tone in any one part will affect the balance of chords. Vibratos must also be uniformly matched throughout.

Low notes   Low notes will frequently need to be played at a slightly higher dynamic level in order to establish a balance. However, this is not always the case. A keen sense of blend and balance dictates how to handle these low notes.

Spread chords   Often, chords are notated situating the trumpets on top, saxes in the middle, and trombones on the bottom. In this case, the trombones will sometimes need to play out a little more to achieve a proper balance. This, of course, depends on the voicing of the chord in that register. Trombones tend to consume a chord (unclear or muddy sounding) if it is voiced very tightly due to the register in which they normally play. Check to see if any notes of the chord are doubled either homogeneously or heterogeneously. If so, be sure to adjust those parts to a proper balance and blend.

Overblowing   Overblowing results in a harsh and unbalanced sound.

An ensemble should strive for a good, solid sound that does not "crack" or "spread" at a high dynamic level. This results in better intonation, balance, and blend. It focuses the sound, which actually penetrates better than a "cracked" or "spread" sound. The main objective of balance and blend is to *listen* and *gain awareness* of other parts. An ensemble can try various seating arrangements in rehearsals to learn how to listen and gain this all-important awareness. Different seating arrangements are found in Chapter 6, "Rehearsal Techniques."

LINE DOMINANCE

Line dominance is knowing which part or parts have the most important line at any given time. All players must be made aware of all the important lines and mark in their part *who* has the dominant line.

Players with dominant lines should concentrate on bringing them out, while players supporting the line should back off a little to allow the dominant line to be heard. In some instances, a fortepiano is written into the supporting parts to accommodate an important line. The players need to get down to the piano immediately and control the crescendo, if there is one, being careful not to swell too soon. (Fig. 1-14)

Figure 1–14. "The Suncatchers" by Marius Nordal, measures 49–50. Copyright 1974 by C. L. Barnhouse Co., Oskaloosa, Iowa 52577.

DYNAMICS

Dynamics found in younger, less experienced bands tend to be tantamount at the mezzo-forte level, moving to an overblown fortissimo at times with very little, if any, contrast present. This is especially true with respect to softer levels. A key word to interesting dynamics is *exaggerate*, particularly in the lower dynamic levels.

One thing that will help ensure proper and interesting dynamics is to develop a good pianissimo concept, making sure to keep a good tempo, pitch, balance, and feel for the music at the same time. After this has been achieved, the fortissimo sections (in contrast) will sound much louder without the unnecessary overblowing.

Every player must pay very close attention to all the markings surrounding the notes. Players must be sure they are playing the proper dynamic levels correctly, bringing out the accents and szforsandos, exaggerating all crescendos and diminuendos, and executing proper fortepianos by exaggerating the immediate softening and controlling the crescendo.

Again the word to remember is *exaggerate*. The entire band, as well as each section, must execute dynamics together, and in the same manner, to prevent a sound that is bland and unexciting.

TEMPO

Tempo is often the factor that can make or break a band in the effectiveness of a performance. A tune played too slowly can create a feeling of ponderous heaviness without any sense of direction and movement to a chart. This is often the mistake made when playing ballads.

At the other extreme, a tune played too quickly can break down the precision vital to a good performance. In fast tunes, set the tempo with respect to the most difficult passages so that no precision is lost.

PRECISION

Precision can be achieved without the performance becoming a mechanistic, stiff endeavor. A chart should have a certain feel of relaxation and flowing to it, while maintaining a strict sense of unity.

Rhythmic precision is one aspect that contributes to this unity. The beat, or pulse, is the important measuring device of rhythms. In problem spots, mark each beat, or pulse, with an arrow. This helps to properly place certain rhythmic figures. It is sometimes helpful when rehearsing to play through the chart slowly, accenting the first note of each grouping of notes. (Fig. 1-15)

Figure 1-15.   "Interlude" by Toshiko Akiyoshi as recorded by the Toshiko Akiyoshi/Lew Tabackin Big Band on the album *Tales of a Courtesan*, RCA #JPLI-0723, measures 78–80 (woodwinds). Copyright 1977 by Toba Publishing Company, distributed by Kendor Music, Inc.

Another area of concern in precision is that of attacks and releases. These should be executed together and in the same manner. (Fig. 1-16)

Figure 1-16

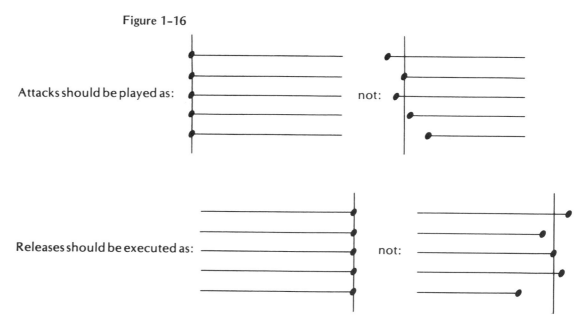

Other areas warranting attention are phrasings and articulations. Again, these must be done in a unified manner. Discussions affecting precision of attacks, releases, articulations, and phrasings are found in Chapters 2 and 3.

To conclude this chapter, I would like to re-emphasize a point. It is necessary for all ensemble members to *listen to* and *follow* the manner of performance of the lead player of their section, or lead trumpet player, in order to achieve a unified and polished performance of the entire ensemble.

Articulations 2

Jazz articulations and phrasings are perhaps the two most difficult concepts to grasp in the jazz idiom, as they vary in idea from person to person, and can be only generalized in their "rules." It therefore stands to reason that only general guidelines and suggestions can be given to help develop a good concept of jazz phrasings and articulations.

Both are extremely interdependent, yet each deserves its own separate treatment. Through the intelligent combination of proper articulations and basic concepts of jazz phrasing, gratifying results will accrue.

There are several types of articulations found in the performance of jazz:

TONGUING

The *legato-tongue* articulation ("D" attack) is the basis of most jazz articulations. The *traditional style* of tonguing ("T" attack) is generally reserved for special effects, such as heavy accents, marcatos, and so forth.

SLURRING

Slurring is done in much the same manner as in the classical sense. The long slur marking does not always denote a phrase to be slurred however. It can serve to inform the player of a certain grouping of notes into a particular phrase. By the same token, the lack of this marking does not necessarily mean that all notes are to be tongued. Knowledge of style and good judgment determine the proper choices of phrasings and articulations in these instances.

Once the legato-tongue articulation has been developed, other specialized types of articulations can be applied to facilitate more effective phrasing and interpretation. These other types include breath articulation, the half-tongue, and the doodle-tongue.

BREATH ARTICULATION

Breath *articulation* or *pushing* is a form of "tonguing" in which the tongue is not actually used. It is produced by a huff from the diaphragm using the syllables "HUH," "HOO," or "WAH." This effect is used in several different instances, one of which is the occurrence of a series of consecutive dotted quarter-eighth figures. In this instance, the breath accent or push, indicated in Fig. 2-1 by the parenthesis for an implied accent, is used and followed by a decay. (Fig. 2-1)

Figure 2–1

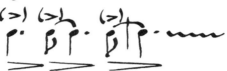

Another possibility for this rhythmic figure is the use of a forte piano attack followed by a crescendo to the next note. (Fig. 2-2)

Figure 2–2

Another application of the breath articulation would be in the appearance of quarter-note triplets. (Fig. 2-3)

Figure 2–3

One of the most common usages of pushing comes in the sustained type of background behind a solo or soli section. Frequently found are a series of half notes under a phrase line. (Fig. 2-4)

Figure 2–4

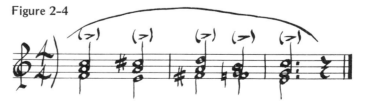

This device becomes especially effective when the various voices move under a sustained figure. (Fig. 2-5)

Figure 2–5. "Back Home" by Sammy Nestico, measure 8 (saxes). Copyright 1961 by Kendor Music, Inc.

The *half-tongue* results in a note that is not clearly tongued or sounded and is produced by a narrowing or partial closing of the mouth cavity with the back of the tongue. This can be achieved by using the syllable "DUD-N" along with a slight breath articulation (actually coming out more like "DUD-HUHN"). Saxes can use the last part of these syllables ("N") to partially stop the vibration of the reed. Valved brass can half-valve slightly to aid the effect. This is applied whenever a "ghosted" or an "x-note" appears, sometimes called "swallowed" notes. A ghosted note is *usually* the lower note in a phrase or group of notes, found mainly in passages of consecutive eighths or triplets, and is indicated by parentheses around the note. (Fig. 2-6)

HALF-TONGUE

Figure 2-6. "Tall Cotton" by Sammy Nestico, as recorded by Count Basie on the album *Basie Big Band*, Pablo #2310-756, measures 38-54 (trumpet 1). Copyright 1976 by Banes Music, Inc.

An x-note is often used interchangeably with a ghosted note. The difference is that the x-note has less definition of pitch. (Fig. 2-7)

The *doodle-tongue* is used to facilitate speed and smoothness in certain passages, primarily triplet figures and fast moving eighth- or sixteenth-note patterns. It is produced by its own phonetic sound, "DOODLE."

DOODLE-TONGUE

A very common practice in playing a string of consecutive eighth notes is to tongue and emphasize every other note on the upbeats, slurring into the downbeats. (Fig. 2-8)

Figure 2-7. "Front Burner" by Sammy Nestico, as recorded by Count Basie on the album *Basie Big Band*, Pablo #2310-756, measures 24–32 (trumpet 1). Copyright 1976 by Banes Music, Inc.

Figure 2-8

Remember that in all tonguing, faster note movement mandates the use of less tongue. This is where incorporation of the breath articulation, half-tongue, doodle-tongue, and the upbeat-slur are extremely useful.

RELEASES   *Releases* are a part of articulation that are often overlooked. With respect to precision, they are of equal importance to attacks in that they too must fit the particular situation and be consistent from person to person at any given time of usage.

Releases are of two basic types. The first is the *breath release* in which the player stops the flow of air through control of the diaphragm. The second is the *tongue release* in which the tongue is used to stop the flow of air. The tongue release can be important for the projection of rhythmic phrases and can stop a tone with almost as much impact as an attack.

The most commonly used articulation markings are as follows:

1. *Horizontal accent* (♩)-Heavy accent, hold note full value.

2. *Vertical (marcato) accent* (♩)-Heavy accent, hold less than full value (hard and short). Sometimes called the "hat" or "roof-top" accent.

3. *Vertical accent with staccato* (♩)-Heavy accent, short as possible (clipped).

4. *Staccato mark* (♩)-Short, not heavy.

5. *Tenuto mark* (♩)-Legato tongue, hold full value.

For a complete listing of articulation markings, see Appendix A.

PHONETICS   Much phrasing can be learned and utilized from scat singing and the phonetics it uses. Many of these phonetics can be used in achieving the proper articulations as they pertain to certain phrases. However, due to certain physical characteristics of some of the "words" in scat singing, modifications must be used for direct application in playing an instrument.

The following are some phonetically spelled articulations which have been applied successfully:

Eighths, quarters, dotted-quarters, halves, dotted-halves, wholes

Marking	"Word"	Where Applied
–	DU	Full value note on the beat or pulse DU DU DU DU DU DU DU DU
–	DUH	Full value note on the up-beat or "and" of a pulse or beat DU DU DU DUH DUH DUH
>	DAH	Full value note with accent or emphasis, any rhythmic placement DUH DU DAH DAH
•	DUHT	Short note with little accent or emphasis, any rhythmic placement; tongue release DU DUH DUHT DUHT DUHT
∧	DAHT	Short note, heavy accent, any rhythmic placement, tongue release DU DAHT DAHT DAHT
∧•	DOT	Very short note (clipped), heavy accent, any rhythmic placement, tongue release DAH DUH DU DOT DOT DOT

Note: *In many instances, the articulation markings are not written but implied because of the general nature of the "rules" of jazz phrasing. This is why a good concept of jazz phrasing is necessary in using this phonetic system.*

Sixteenths (played "straight")

DU DEE DUH DUH

Triplets (played "straight")

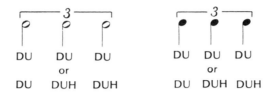

DU	DU	DU
	or	
DU	DUH	DUH

DU	DU	DU
	or	
DU	DUH	DUH

Using breath accents (pushing):

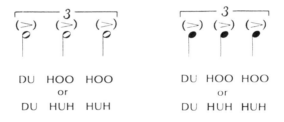

DU	HOO	HOO
	or	
DU	HUH	HUH

DU	HOO	HOO
	or	
DU	HUH	HUH

Eighth note triplets:

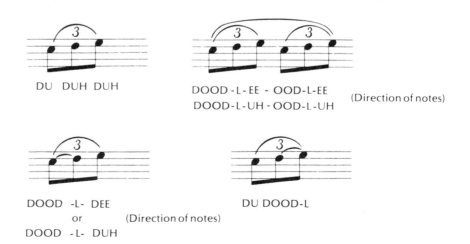

DU DUH DUH

DOOD - L - EE - OOD - L - EE
DOOD - L - UH - OOD - L - UH   (Direction of notes)

DOOD -L- DEE
     or   (Direction of notes)
DOOD -L- DUH

DU DOOD-L

Half-tonguing (the "N" represents the half-tongued note)

"Word"	Where Applied
DUD—N	Used when a phrase or group of notes contain a "swallowed" note 
DAHD—N	The note preceding the half-tongue is full value and accented 
DUHT—N	The note preceding the half-tongue is short with little or no emphasis 
DAHT—N	The note preceding the half-tongue is short and accented 
DOT—N	The note preceding the half-tongue is very short (clipped) and accented 

Note: *As mentioned before, the "N" in half-tonguing is actually more like "HUHN" by virtue of a slight breath articulation. Again, jazz phrasing may only imply a "swallowed" note, and it is up to the player to decide when to use the half-tongue.*

Half-tonguing triplets

Slurs

DU - EE
or
DAH - EE

DU - AH
or
DAH - AH

DUH-
OO   DUH-   DUH-   DUH-   DUH - OO
     OO   OO   OO
or   DAH-   DAH-   DAH-   DAH-   DAH - OO
     OO   OO   OO   OO

Special effects

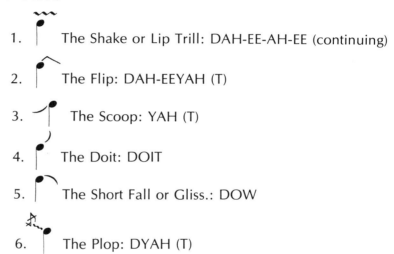

1. The Shake or Lip Trill: DAH-EE-AH-EE (continuing)

2. The Flip: DAH-EEYAH (T)

3. The Scoop: YAH (T)

4. The Doit: DOIT

5. The Short Fall or Gliss.: DOW

6. The Plop: DYAH (T)

Syncopations

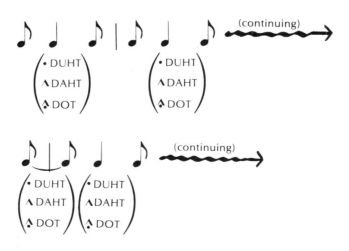

(• DUHT)
(∧ DAHT)
(▲ DOT)

(• DUHT)
(∧ DAHT)
(▲ DOT)

(continuing)

(• DUHT)
(∧ DAHT)
(▲ DOT)

(• DUHT)
(∧ DAHT)
(▲ DOT)

(continuing)

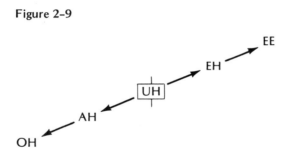

Longer duration notes - written or implied accent or emphasis

As registers change, some slight modifications of these syllables can be made. The higher registers can go more to an "EH" or "EE" sound, while the lower ones can move more toward an "AH" or "OH" sound. (Fig. 2-9)

Figure 2–9

Remember that the most effective phrasing is a result of mixing the different articulations and releases available to the player. They must be appropriate to, and consistent with, a good concept of jazz phrasing.

Following is an example of phonetics as applied to an actual piece of music. It has been approached as if every note were articulated. In a true performance, slurring, traditional-style tonguing, and so on would be mixed into the phrasing. The purpose is to give examples of the proper articulation of these figures as if they were isolated from the "mixed" interpretation of articulations. (It is sometimes helpful for students to write in the "words" on a piece of music they are currently working with to aid in the understanding of proper phrasing). (Fig. 2-10)

Figure 2–10. "Studio 'J'" by Toshiko Akiyoshi as recorded by the Toshiko Akiyoshi/Lew Tabackin Big Band on the album *Insights*, RCA #AFL1-2678, measures 17–33 (lead trumpet). Copyright 1978 by Newport Music Company, distributed by Kendor Music, Inc.

Phrasings 3

Jazz phrasing might best be described as an individualistic concept contained in each person's mind. The following discussion will hopefully provide a common denominator for musicians to enable them to work together in arriving at a unified goal.

The most problematic concept to be learned is the interpretation of eighth-note figures in swing-style playing.

EIGHTH NOTES

In a series of two or more consecutive eighth notes, a two-thirds to one-third ratio of note value is the closest interpretation. Specifically, a triplet or twelve-eight feel prevails. (Fig. 3-1)

Figure 3-1

Written:

Played:

Another figure sometimes used to indicate a swing feel is the dotted eighth, sixteenth pattern. It is not to be played literally but with the same interpretation as the swung eighth notes. The rhythmic subdivision is as follows (Fig. 3-2):

Figure 3-2

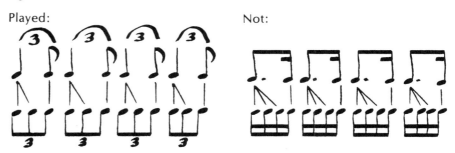

This figure is often used to delineate the difference of desired feel in a chart that has had a straight eighth-note pattern as a basis of interpretation. A good example of this occurs in Marius Nordal's *Fancy*[1] in which the chart is basically a Bossa Nova with the contrasting swing feel written in the dotted eighth, sixteenth manner, occuring in measures 54–55, 79–80, 86–88, 101, 103, 111–113, and 117–121.

However, it must not be taken for granted that the dotted eighth, sixteenth pattern is always swung. Sometimes the "ricky-ticky" effect is desired, in which case every note would be played short and in an exaggerated staccato manner. (Fig. 3-3)

Figure 3-3

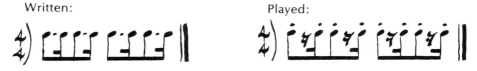

There are, however, a few exceptions to swinging the eighth-note patterns.

Eighth notes are played "straight" or "even" when playing Latin American music, most rock charts, many ballads (at least much closer to even eighths), waltzes, jazz waltzes, and fast bop or progressive jazz. (These styles will be discussed more later.)

A series of consecutive eighth notes leading into a climax or melody will be phrased evenly when marked with marcato accents (hat accents). For further clarification, this is sometimes indicated with the words "straight," "even," or "st." (Fig. 3-4)

[1]Oskaloosa, IA: C. L. Barnhouse Co., 1975.

Figure 3-4

Isolated eighth notes, eighths tied over the bar, tied eighth notes, and a phrase ending with an eighth note should all be played short and accented to some extent. (Fig. 3-5)

Figure 3-5

On a series of consecutive eighth notes of the same pitch, the first and last notes receive emphasis and a crescendo runs through the pattern. (Fig. 3-6)

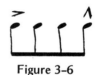

Figure 3-6

When the pattern begins on the second or fourth beat, the accents will fall on the first of each two eighth notes. (Fig. 3-7)

Figure 3-7

Sometimes, melodic lines will have accents on the upbeats, a device that can be employed to enhance a line in slow to medium-fast tempos. In this instance, a light legato tongue, breath accents (pushing), or a combination of the two is applied to the upbeats. (Fig. 3-8)

Figure 3-8. "Back Home" by Sammy Nestico, measures 1–8 (melody line, lead alto). Copyright 1961 by Kendor Music, Inc.

EXCEPTIONS TO SWINGING EIGHTH NOTES

As mentioned earlier in this chapter, there are exceptions to swinging eighth notes. One of the most prominent areas is in the field of rock or jazz/rock. The history of jazz has developed along many lines and the influences of rock during the fifties and sixties can be seen in the music of the seventies and on into the eighties.

One of the main reasons why rock elements were integrated into jazz with relative ease is that, conversely, rock has drawn nearly all its elements from jazz—and especially from blues, the spirituals, gospel songs and the popular music of the black ghetto, rhythm and blues. Here, the symmetrical, steady rock beat, the gospel and soul phrases, the blues form and blues sound, the penetrating sound of the electric guitar, etc. had all been in existence long before the appearance of rock. Shelly Manne, the drummer, once said: "If jazz borrows from rock, it only borrows from itself."[2]

With charts that are in the *rock or jazz/rock* style, the rhythms are played exactly as written. The styling and interpretation is determined by the articulation applied to the rhythms. Generally, notes of short duration will be played in a quasi-staccato to staccato manner. Tongue releases will be used more frequently than in other types of charts. Many of the newer charts include the articulation markings for the desired effects. The following examples show various rhythms and articulations common to rock and jazz/rock music (Figs. 3-9 to 3-11):

Figure 3-9. "Mother Fingers" by Pete Jackson as recorded by Maynard Ferguson on the album *M. F. Horn III*, Columbia #KC-32403, measures D-E (sketch score). Copyright 1973 by Destructive World Music, all rights reserved.

[2]Joachim Berendt, *The Jazz Book, From New Orleans to Rock and Free Jazz*, trans. Dan Morgenstern, Helmut and Barbara Bredigkeit (Westport, Conn.: Lawrence Hill and Co., Inc., 1975), pp. 47-48.

Figure 3-10. "Awright, Awright" by Pete Jackson as recorded by Maynard Ferguson on the album *M. F. Horn III*, Columbia #KC-32403, measures 29–44 (trumpet and flute). Copyright 1973 by Destructive World Music, all rights reserved.

Figure 3-11. "Goober's New Dune Boogey" by Henry Wolking, measures A-A[1] (soli line). Copyright 1975 by Southern Music Company, San Antonio, Texas 78292. Used by permission.

Rhythmic figures in *Latin* tunes are likewise played exactly as written. The styling and interpretation are determined by the articulations used. They are smoother, with a more flowing approach. Long, even strings of syncopated quarter notes are frequently used in the bossa nova melodies. They should be played full value (tenuto) as opposed to the short interpretation found in the jazz style. Rhythmic background figures in the rhythm section help to determine the proper styling differences. Latin music consists of many different background rhythms including the samba, rhumba, cha-cha, mambo, bossa nova, and more. The delineations of these will be further discussed in Chapter 4, "The Rhythm Section." Following is an example of Latin music (Fig. 3-12):

Figure 3-12. "Samba De Haps" by Mark Taylor, measures 31-56 (flute, alto, flugelhorn). Copyright 1976 by New Bentley Music Co., published by Creative World Music Publications.

Ballads are played in several styles. One ballad can have a swing feel, while another can be played "straight" (eighth notes played evenly). Generally, they are played smoothly throughout, with a lot of slurring or legato-tongue being used. Phrase markings are more likely to be found written into the parts. (Fig. 3-13)

Figure 3-13. "Another Time, Another Place" by Don Schamber, measures 8-16 (solo trumpet). Copyright 1974 by DVS Publications. Used by permission.

Waltzes, especially *jazz waltzes,* are played very smooth and evenly. A jazz waltz is usually played one beat per measure or with a six-eight feel covering two bars. Long, flowing phrases are characteristic of a jazz waltz. Following is such an example (Fig. 3-14):

Figure 3-14. "La Fiesta" by Chick Corea, arranged by Tony Klatka as recorded by the Woody Herman Orchestra on the album *Giant Steps,* Fantasy F-9432, measures 8-25 (lead alto). Copyright 1976 by Litha Music Co., published by Warner Bros.

Because of the tempo of fast *bop* music, rhythmic figures, especially eighth notes, must be played very close to even and exact. The styling is a result of articulations and specific placement of accents on certain notes. Some examples of bop tunes would include "Ko Ko," "Donna Lee," "Ornithology," "Groovin High," and "Straight, No Chaser."

Quarter notes, whether on the beat or syncopated, are played shorter than full value unless otherwise notated by a tenuto mark, staccato mark, hat accent, or other mark. They would receive two-thirds the normal value. (Fig. 3-15)

Two things should be mentioned here. First, the faster the tempo, the shorter the quarter note should be played. Second, care should be taken that the quarter notes are not played too short in "laid-back" tunes. (A laid-back tune is one which is played at a slower tempo with a much more relaxed feel or manner.) In other words, the shortness, or length, of quarter notes is dictated by the tempo.

Generally, anything greater in time value than a quarter note will receive full value. These include dotted quarters, halves, dotted halves, and wholes, or their equivalents due to ties.

The use of crescendos and diminuendos are ways of adding interest, avoiding a sound that lays flat in slower tempos or longer note valued phrases. (Fig. 3-16)

QUARTER NOTES

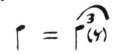

Figure 3-15

FULL VALUE NOTES

Figure 3–16

Depending on the tune and overall styling, another effective device is the fortepiano, followed by a swell or crescendo to the release or next attack. (Releases are discussed later in this chapter.) (Fig. 3-17)

Figure 3–17

As mentioned in the previous chapter, long and sustained background figures can be pushed (breath articulation) to create interest. (See Figs. 2-4 and 2-5.)

DOTTED-QUARTER NOTES

Special attention is given to the dotted-quarter note as it can fall into the category of full-value notes and/or syncopations, the next subject of discussion.

Figure 3–18

A series of consecutive, tied dotted quarters and eighths could be played any one of three main ways. The first way is for all notes to receive no special treatment. (Fig. 3-18)

Figure 3–19

Secondly, it could receive a forte piano treatment followed by a swell or crescendo to the point of release or next attack. (Fig. 3-19)

The third way incorporates breath articulations, wherein each note is pushed and followed by a decay to the point of release or next attack. (Fig. 3-20)

Figure 3–20

When an eighth note comes at the end of a measure preceded by a dotted-quarter note, or its equivalent, it is very important to place the eighth note before the next downbeat without rushing it. The eighth note is almost always accented or emphasized in some manner. (Fig. 3-21)

Figure 3–21

The avoidance of rushing is achieved with a delay of the eighth note by conceiving it in triplet form. (Figs. 3-22A and 3-22B)

Figure 3–22a

Written: Played:

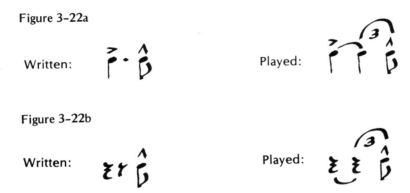

Figure 3–22b

Written: Played:

Another similar figure is the dotted quarter followed by an eighth that is tied to a longer valued note. Again, the eighth note receives the triplet delay as before. (Figs. 3-23A and 3-23B)

Figure 3–23a

Written: Played:

Figure 3–23b

Written: Played:

The "kick beat," a dotted-quarter note immediately preceding a bar line, is always sustained and accented, or emphasized, to some extent. Take care not to rush or anticipate this figure. As in the previous cases, the the triplet delay is used, this time falling on beat three. (Fig. 3-24)

Written: [musical notation] Played: [musical notation]

Figure 3-24

SYNCOPATIONS A good general "rule" would be to always shorten a syncopated note. Some exceptions to this would be when the note value is more than a quarter note; when it is marked with a tenuto mark or phrase line; and when it is not characteristic of the style of the chart being played.

One of the most commonly found syncopations is the eighth-quarter-eighth figure. The first eighth note is played long; the quarter note is played short. The second eighth is played short unless it is a continuing figure, in which case it would be played long. (Figs. 3-25A and 3-25B)

Figure 3-25a

Written: [musical notation] Marked: [musical notation] Played: [musical notation]

Figure 3-25b

Written: [musical notation] Marked: [musical notation] Played: [musical notation]

When the eighth-quarter-eighth figure appears in a tune that is using straight eighths, as in a rock chart, the long-short styling is usually reversed. (Fig. 3-26)

Figure 3-26

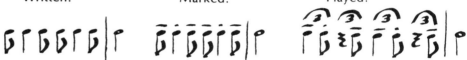

Another type is the syncopation across a bar line. (Fig. 3-27)

Figure 3-27

Written: [musical notation] Marked: [musical notation] Played: [musical notation]

One of the most difficult of syncopated figures is the occurrence of consecutive syncopated quarter notes. Placement of the triplet delay is the key factor. (Figs. 3-28A and 3-28B)

Figure 3–28a

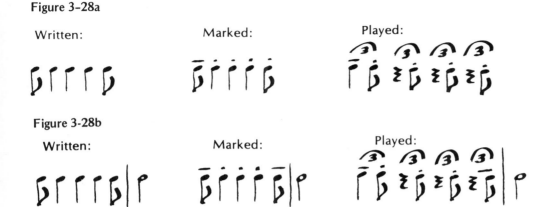

Figure 3-28b

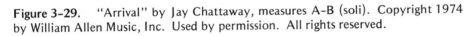

Another aspect of creating interest and movement in a chart is that of line contouring. Simply put, it is the application of accents and dynamics to fit the directional movement of the notes in a phrase or phrases. The highest note and last note of a phrase receive accents or emphasis; an ascending phrase is played with a slight crescendo, and a descending phrase is played with a slight diminuendo. (Fig. 3-29)

LINE CONTOURING

Figure 3-29.   "Arrival" by Jay Chattaway, measures A–B (soli). Copyright 1974 by William Allen Music, Inc. Used by permission. All rights reserved.

RELEASES The basic consideration with releases is that they must be done together and in the same manner. As mentioned before, the two types of releases are the *breath* (diaphragm) release and the *tongue* release. Generally, short isolated notes incorporate the tongue release, while longer notes use the breath release. This does not necessarily mean that one type of release cannot be used in the reverse situation.

A general guideline to placement of releases is to sustain a note full value if it is followed by some sort of rest or break. (Fig. 3-30)

Figure 3–30

In the case of longer duration notes where there is no rest or break in between, a release can be inserted as long as it is not overused. (Fig. 3-31)

Figure 3–31

It is sometimes necessary to release a note short of its time value at the end of a phrase when something immediately follows. (Fig. 3-32)

Figure 3–32

One particular point of confusion arises in the case of an eighth note that is tied to the previous note. It may mean either to hold the note an extra half-beat or it may just serve to indicate that the preceding note should be played at its full value. (Figs. 3-33A and 3-33B)

Figure 3–33a   Figure 3–33b

It is up to the director or lead player of the section or ensemble to determine the type of release and placement to be used in each situation.

Variations in style and phrasing must be analyzed as to the characteristic of a particular kind of music, composer, band, time period, and so on for proper and idiomatic playing of the music.

VARIATIONS IN STYLE AND PHRASING

The term "swing" has as many definitions as it has people trying to define it. It is made up of two basic things: *interpretation* and *unity*. Coker gives his views and ideas on the subject in his book, *Improvising Jazz.*

> The intensity of swing can vary greatly in the styles of different jazz musicians—indeed, it can even vary at times within a single individual. The tunes and arrangements can also call for more or less intensity of swing. Intensity of swing can be determined by any one, or a combination of these factors: (1) dynamic level or loudness; (2) mood or time-feeling; (3) unity in the sense that all members of a performing group are playing with the same concept of the pulse. With these variables, it is easy to see how individual tastes might conflict on such an issue.[3]

For the most part, the discussion in this chapter has dealt with the more common styles that are currently being written and played. The following contains brief descriptions of other styles associated with jazz and its development.

Swing Early *swing* had slight variations of phrasing, including the crisper clipping off of notes and a shorter style of staccato. *Up-tempo swing* has the constant feel of driving forward without rushing the beat. *Laid-back swing* has the feel of holding back, playing almost behind the beat, without dragging. The pulse remains constant in all of these.

Bop Bop is characterized by fast tempos, fast chord progressions, uncommon chord sequences, complex chord structures, and longer solos containing more of a steady stream of notes. Because of the faster tempos, eighth-note patterns are played very close to even, using accents and articulations to shape the phrases.

Dixieland Dixieland has very much the same interpretation as swing, except that it is characterized by the accenting of beats two and four by the rhythm section. (This is commonly called "two-beat" background.)

Ballads Ballads generally are phrased smoothly, with the eighth notes played evenly or nearly so. Fuller tone and vibrato are present along with more sustaining qualities throughout.

[3]Jerry Coker, *Improvising Jazz* (Englewood Cliffs, NJ: Prentice-Hall, Inc., © 1964), p. 45.

Latin Music In *Latin American* music, the eighth notes are played straight, with the accents and staccatos played very accurately. The most difficult task is to distinguish between the many different types of background rhythms, such as the Samba, Rhumba, Mambo, and Bossa Nova. (See Chapter 4.)

Waltzes *Waltzes* and *Jazz Waltzes* contain very smooth lines and are played evenly.

Polkas *Polkas* are always counted in cut-time, having two beats to the measure falling on the strong beats. The phrasing is even, and a heavier style of tonguing is used.

Rock and Funk Finally, *Rock* and *Funk* music have their own stylings peculiar to them. They are generally played in a strict sense as in Latin American music and are more angular in nature. In fact, much of rock and funk music show a great deal of Latin influence.

A little more detailed discussion of these various styles can be found in *Developmental Techniques for the Jazz Ensemble Musician*[4] by Rev. George Wiskirchen, C.S.C. Another source of information on jazz phrasing is *The Interpretation of the Jazz Language*[5] by Clark Terry and Phil Rizzo.

At this point, reviewing the previous chapter on articulations would perhaps be beneficial. Some clarification and unification of certain points might result.

[4]Boston, MA: Berklee Press Publications, 1961.
[5]Bedford, Ohio: M.A.S. Publishing Company, 1978.

The Rhythm Section 4

The rhythm section is unique in that its members provide more than just a rhythmic background for other players. Collectively, the members of a rhythm section possess a three-fold ability to function: (1) rhythmic background; (2) harmonic background; and (3) solos. They can perform as a completely separate unit apart from a big band containing horns, yet sound full and complete.

The rhythm section, more than any one other section of an ensemble, has the most problems in achieving its purpose. This is especially true with respect to proper styling. It is not necessarily the absolute fault of the players in the section though. Oftentimes, the director of a jazz ensemble may be a "legitimately" trained *wind* player, with a background of only one or two courses in percussion techniques, strings, and piano. The director may or may not have had any exposure to jazz techniques, and if so, it may have only come through participation in a jazz group. Another thing adding to the difficulties of learning about styles is that the younger players are exposed more to pop and rock through the radio than to the various styles found in the jazz idiom. Most rock charts are relatively easy for the rhythm section to grasp because of this exposure. However, this is limited to the easier rock rhythms that are often found in rock and pop on the radio. There are, however, very complex rock charts that need the attention and study required of other jazz forms.

It therefore stands to reason that the rhythm section demands the respect of equality, purpose, and function comparable, if not more so, to the horns.

The basic make-up of a rhythm section includes drums, bass, piano, and guitar. Each of these will be discussed defining their functions within the ensemble both individually and as a unit.

DRUMS Historically, the drummer has been given the label of "timekeeper." While this still holds true to a great extent, the manner in which this is achieved has changed through the years. Early drummers relied on the bass drum to keep the time, playing on every beat. This progressed into the Swing Era when the pulse was switched more to the cymbals, away from the bass drum, which then was used mainly for accenting purposes. Also taking place at this time was the shift from accenting all four beats, or one and three, to the second and fourth beats, and was played on the hi-hat cymbals.

From here, the Bop Era developed on this style, using the accented two and four, and adding (1) *fills* (improvised rhythms played during short rests or "holes"; (2) *set-ups* (rhythmic figures preceding an ensemble entrance that helps the ensemble to "feel" their entrance); and (3) *kicks* or *bombs* (very heavy accents).

Melodic aspects began to be explored throughout, especially during solos, finally giving way more toward *percussive* melodies. Through the use of relatively recent developments in electronic sound altering devices and variable-pitch drums, the melodic aspect has again taken on new light.

Newer jazz, or "free form," took on an "implied beat." The pulse was felt by the members of the group without the drummer having to play a structured time pattern. This is found mainly in smaller group situations.

For most playing at present, the pulse is maintained on a ride cymbal, hi-hats, or both, reserving the bass drum, snare, and toms for accents. Rock charts require a similar method of playing, only using the drums themselves more frequently and in a much heavier manner.

The modern working drummer will at times be faced with having to play many tempos and styles. Therefore, the drummer must study and *practice* all the styles of the past and present and know them inside out.

As previously mentioned, the pulse is established on the cymbals in the form of a "ride rhythm." Following are a few basic examples of ride rhythms found in some of the different styles.

The *swing* style is the most widely used and the pattern is played somewhat relaxed. (Fig. 4-1)

Written:

Played:

Figure 4–1

In a *slow ballad* or *blues,* a variation of this can be played that incorporates quarter notes along with the dotted eighth-sixteenth figure. (Fig. 4-2)

Figure 4–2

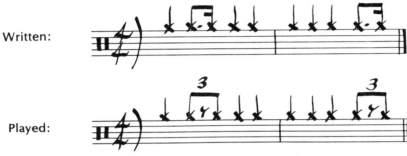

Written:

Played:

In a *shuffle* or *dixieland* context, the figure will be played as written. (Fig. 4-3)

Figure 4–3

Written and Played:

In *up-tempo* tunes, regardless of how the ride rhythm is notated, the eighth notes are played very evenly. (Fig. 4-4)

Figure 4–4

Played:

In some instances, a drummer may wish to play straight quarter notes for a more driving effect. (Fig. 4-5)

Figure 4-5

Played:

The drummer may wish to combine the two in various ways. (Fig. 4-6)

Figure 4-6

Played :   (a)

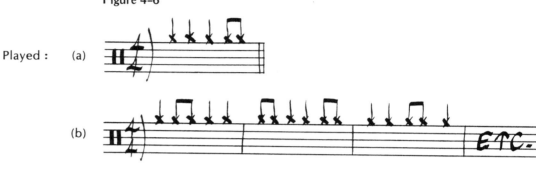

(b)

(c)   Make your own combinations.

In *Latin* tunes, straight eighth notes played evenly set the style and pulse. (Fig. 4-7)

Figure 4-7

Written and Played:

The same is basically true for *Rock* ride rhythms. Beats two and four are accented more often. (Fig. 4-8)

Figure 4-8

Played:

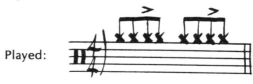

Other common ride rhythms found in rock are sixteenths and the basic "disco beat." (Figs. 4-9A and 4-9B)

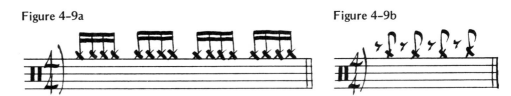

Figure 4–9a   Figure 4–9b

Note: the disco beat is played on a partially closed hi-hat.

In *triple-feel* meters (three-four, six-eight, twelve-eight, and so on), the number of ride rhythms are many, and their combinations are almost limitless. Again, the eighths are played evenly. These are just a few. (Fig. 4-10)

Figure 4–10

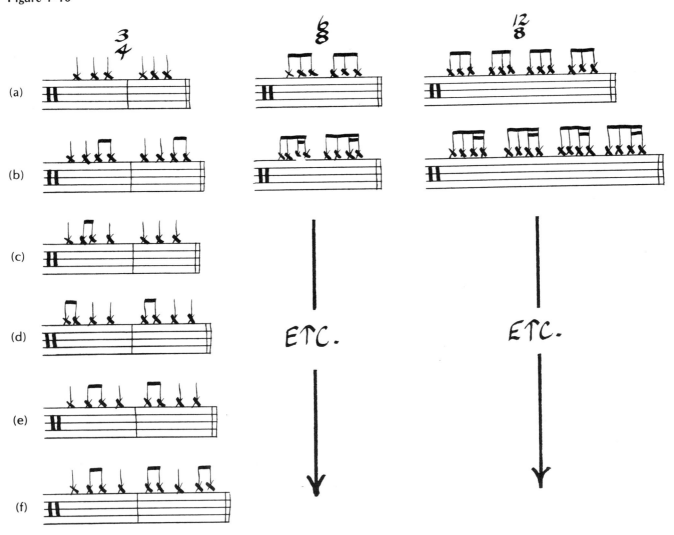

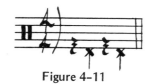

Figure 4-11

When playing straight time, the *hi-hat* is normally played on beats two and four in a four-four time meter (open on one and three; closed on two and four). (Fig. 4-11)

Of course, there are many variations available to the drummer, especially in three-four jazz or odd meters.

The *bass drum* should be used sparingly, mostly for accents and kicks. In a big band situation, the bass drum can be played very lightly on all beats to underline the bass. But the drummer must be very careful not to be "heard," but rather "felt."

The *snare drum* will usually be used for accenting and playing ensemble rhythmic figures. The *tom-toms* can be used for accents, special effects, and fills.

Reading drum set music is a must for a player in a large ensemble. Drum charts are often just written as a sketch part in which the drummer must use his or her knowledge of good set playing to create an interesting part. Because of this freedom, the drummer must keep in mind not to play too busily. Remember that the drummer's basic function is to keep time and punctuate ensemble figures.

If the written drum part is too sketchy, the drummer may wish to look at the score or the lead horn parts, especially the lead trumpet part, and pencil in the important rhythmic figures that need to be punctuated. Also, be sure to mark all dynamics. Most importantly, listen to what is happening throughout the entire ensemble. Try to enhance the sound and not detract from it because of an uneducated approach.

Fills are sometimes indicated in a drum part when the ensemble has a short rest or break. A fill, essentially, is a short solo that fills the space and sets up the next ensemble entrance. Nothing very intricate should be played as a fill if it could confuse the ensemble as to when to re-enter. Reserve the intricate playing for a solo of longer duration.

When a part indicates a drum solo, drummers have more opportunity to stretch out and show a little more of what they have (sometimes have not) got. They must keep in mind that the solo should not be just a show of how fast and how many drums you can play, but rather make a musically valid statement in keeping with the character of the music being played. Following are some examples of drum parts. (Figs. 4-12A and 4-12B)

The first example is a part that contains several different indications as to what the drummer should be playing at the various spots in the music. At letter "A," a straight time pattern is called for with the measure before "B" being written to emphasize a brass figure, returning to the time pattern at "B." Letter "C" is written in a manner that punctuates what is being played by the ensemble and includes a one bar fill. Again at "D," time is indicated with a set-up written two bars before "E." Letter "E" is a mixture of time patterns, ensemble punctuations, and fills, eventually returning to the time pattern again.

Figure 4–12a. "Basie Straight Ahead" by Sammy Nestico, recorded by Count Basie and his Orchestra on the album *Basie Straight Ahead*, Dot DLP 25902. Copyright 1968 by Banes Music, Inc., Kendor Music, Inc., sole selling agent.

The next example also indicates certain rhythmic figures that the horns are playing. At measures 1, 17, 33, and 48 the indication is to play a standard samba rhythm. Again at 65, the background horn figures are supplied to be used as a guide to punctuations.

Figure 4–12b. "Warning! Success May Be Hazardous to Your Health" by Toshiko Akiyoshi, recorded by the Toshiko Akiyoshi-Lew Tabackin Big Band on the album *Road Time*, RCA No. CPL2-2242. Copyright 1977 by Toba Publishing Company, distributed by Kendor Music, Inc.

The equipment a drummer uses reflects personal tastes and interests just as horn players have their own particular preferences toward their instruments. The basic drum set will usually consist of a snare drum, small ride tom-tom, large floor tom-tom, and a bass drum. In addition to the drums themselves, many combinations of cymbals are added.

Generally speaking, smaller drums will be used in combo situations and larger drums with the bigger ensembles. Different sizes and numbers of drums and cymbals can be added to a set for greater variation of available sounds.

The tuning of a set of drums has a great deal to do with getting a certain sound: Any good drummer knows that it is important to tune the drums to fit the particular sound of the group he or she is working with. Drummers must consider the type and size of group, its style, and the place of performance. Rock drummers, for example, will usually tune their drums down somewhat and use a lot of muffling to produce a deader sound. On the other hand, most jazz drummers want a more open sound, one in which the drums have a little ring to them.

Various methods of muffling can be used to achieve the sound a drummer desires. One of the most common methods has been to use a narrow strip of cloth across the inside of the drum head, held in place by the head and rim. (Fig. 4-13)

Figure 4-13

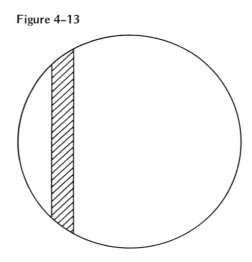

Some drummers will put pillows, blankets, or wadded-up paper in their bass drum to achieve muffling. Another means of muffling can be used in emergency situations when time does not permit any other method, that of taping the drums.

Perhaps the best approach with the bass drum, since it is the one drum needing the most attention, is the method of *centered-sound* muffling. Several types of material can be used; however, a fine muslin cloth is probably best suited for this.

On the batter side, cover the area except where the pedal would strike. It should be about the size of the black dot on a Remo C.S. head. (Fig. 4-14)

Figure 4-14

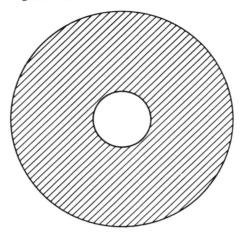

On the front head, use about a two-inch strip around the head. (Fig. 4-15)

Figure 4-15

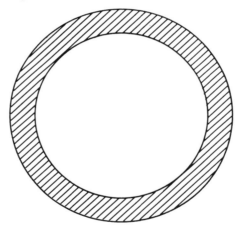

Another means of creating different sounds is to remove the bottom heads from the tom-toms and the front head of the bass drum. The best thing to do is to listen, experiment, and then do whatever is appropriate for any given situation. It is not good to accept one method of tuning and let it apply toward every situation. Have several general tunings and adjust as needed.

One of the traditional ways of tuning a drum, using both heads, is to tune the batter side a little tighter than the opposite side. Some flexibility and control can be gained by doing just the opposite though, as well as getting a sound more conducive to the jazz and rock styles. Again, experiment until you have reached the desired sound and feel for your needs and purposes. Fine tuning can be achieved by lightly pressing the head in the center with the thumb and tapping the head near the rim at each tension rod. The sound should be the same all the way around. If the pitch is low, tighten that tension rod; if it is high, loosen the tension rod. Do this in a crossing manner, tuning opposite tension rods.

Periodically change heads as they lose some of their sound and tone after some time. Also check the snares, lubricate the tension rods, and clean the rims thoroughly. If you take care of your equipment, it should last for a long time.

The most personal part of any drummer's set is the cymbals. They come in all styles, sizes, and weights. There are several brands today that are of good quality. In choosing your cymbals, it is very important to test and compare. Compare not only brand against brand, but cymbal against cymbal so that it does not sustain too long or have too much overring.

The sizes and thicknesses must be chosen carefully for what they are to be used for. No matter in what context a drummer is working, there must be a variety of cymbals for different sounds and effects. Sound response has to be taken into account also. Thin cymbals, when struck, give a fast response whereas a medium to heavy cymbal will have a slightly delayed response.

Hi-hat cymbals usually have a heavier bottom cymbal than the top to produce a good clean "chick" sound upon closing. Most hi-hat stands will have an adjustable tilter for the bottom cymbal to vary how quickly the cymbals close, thereby producing different sounds.

A *ride cymbal,* sometimes called a *ping cymbal,* should be a fairly heavy cymbal so that it does not sustain too long or have too much overring. Clarity is a key factor in selecting and using a ride cymbal. The size of bell or cup of a cymbal can determine the degree of clarity. The smaller the cup, the more clarity of sound. Some cymbals have what is called a mini-cup, and others, such as the flat-top, have no cup at all.

A *crash cymbal* should fall within the medium-thin range of weights. It should sound like a strong crash with a quick decay or dying away of sound.

A *splash cymbal* will have very little duration of sound. Most splash cymbals used are small and thin with a very high pitch.

Another cymbal coming into more common usage now is the *swish-knocker cymbal,* which is designed like the old Chinese cymbals with the turned-up ends. It is sometimes used as a ride cymbal.

Rivets may be added to a cymbal to get a sizzle effect which acts as a sustaining device.

The choice of sticks is another factor the drummer must work with in arriving at proper sound and style. Small jazz work will usually use light, fairly small sticks, whereas rock will use heavier and larger sticks. There are all kinds and sizes of grips (shafts) and beads (heads or tips) available. Among the choices of beads are the wood-tip, nylon-tip, metal-tip, and in some instances, no tip at all. All metal sticks are also available. The drummer should experiment with the different types and use them to suit the various needs. Be careful to avoid warped sticks, which easily can be determined by rolling them across any flat surface.

Auxiliary rhythm parts are included in some charts, especially those written in a Latin style. Drummers should know the techniques of playing the various auxiliary percussion instruments, among them: bongos, congas, maracas, guiros, cabasas, claves, cowbells, and more. These instruments can each produce many sounds that can add a great deal of color to a chart if played properly.

In addition to auxiliary percussion parts, vibe parts are occasionally written, most often as a solo doubling of some horn part. The person who plays vibes could possibly be a second percussionist for the ensemble that plays the auxiliary percussion parts mentioned above.

In quick review, the drummer's main duty is toward keeping good time, using the proper rhythmic patterns, fills, set-ups, and accents that will add to the excitement of a chart, whether it is behind an entire ensemble or soloist. Using equipment that is right for one situation might not be for another. Use different drums tuned properly for whatever context you are to be playing in. Also, vary the sizes, types, and thicknesses of cymbals to be used in these differing situations. Learn and practice all the auxiliary instruments so that they may be used properly and effectively. Work as a part of the whole ensemble rather than as just an individual. Last, but not least, listen intently to what others are doing, especially professional players, and make continual adjustments to fit appropriately into each situation.

BASS   The bass is the most important member of the rhythm section for two reasons. Its function is to (1) be the primary pulse setter, and (2) outline the harmonic basis of the band. It would be much easier for a band to function without drums than without a bass.

The bass player has the responsibility of maintaining an absolutely solid, steady beat, and at the same time providing a "feeling" of pushing ahead, in a fast tempo, or laying back, at a slower tempo, while never varying the pulse even the slightest.

Two types of basses are used in playing the music prevalent to today's music scene: (1) the traditional upright acoustic string bass, and (2) the electric bass guitar. Very rarely will you find an unamplified acoustic string bass being used, especially with big band work. Several very good acoustic pickups or transducers are available to the string bass player, among them, Polytone and Barcus-Berry. The electric bass made its impact with the rock bands of the fifties, and due to this impact more and more jazz musicians eventually turned to it because of its strong supporting bass lines.

The use of both instruments is an ideal situation. The amplified acoustic bass fits the character and style of most jazz charts whereas the electric bass is more suited to the rock charts. Of course, either could be used exclusively if only one were available to the bass player. Hopefully, most schools provide access to both.

Written arrangements sometimes will specify "string bass" or "electric bass," or may simply say "bass." When neither is specified, be sure to analyze the style and mood of the piece in selecting which bass to use.

Bass parts are written in several different manners. The first way contains written notes only. This is found most often in charts written for younger players. A second way contains only chord symbols. This is more prevalent in advanced charts where the bass player is expected to interpret the symbols and improvise a good bass line. The third way combines the first two, written notes and chord symbols. When this third way appears, the written notes are usually an important part of the harmonic structure desired by the arranger or composer and should be played as written, leaving the improvised lines for realizing the chord symbols.

In order to improvise a good bass line, the player must have a solid foundation in the knowledge of scales, modes, and chords. The two major types of bass lines are (1) *chordal* (arpeggiated), and (2) *scalular* ("walking bass").

The first method is much easier for beginners to start working with in improvising a line. The important notes of a chord (1,3,5, sometimes 7 or a flatted 7) should be used, with emphasis given to the roots and fifths. Following is an example of this type of bass line (Fig. 4-16):

Figure 4-16

The walking line takes a much smoother and flowing linear approach. Non-chord tones (dissonant tones) are used to fill between the chord tones. This usually falls on beats 2 and 4. These non-chord tones include notes within the scale built on the chord root, and chromatic tones (notes not within the key). This method provides a much better bass line than the first. A few skips and leaps (chordal) can be incorporated, but the idea is to try to maintain the diatonic and chromatic approach for the majority of the time. Faster tempo tunes are more likely to use non-chord tones as a part of the bass line than slower tempo tunes. Following is an example of a walking bass line (Fig. 4-17):

Figure 4-17

Whatever style bass line is being used, utilize mainly the lower and middle registers of the bass for the most part, especially with the walking line. Incorporate the upper register during solo work, but do not use it exclusively for that purpose.

Rhythmically speaking, the bass line should mostly be a simple pattern of quarter notes and occasional eighth-note patterns. Once in awhile, the bass will play a *two-beat* background, one in which the root is usually played on beat one, and the fifth on beat three, resting on beats two and four. If the chords change on beats one and three, the bass will then play just the roots of those chords. Bass parts in rock charts will tend to be somewhat more complex rhythmically and harmonically, taking on more angular characteristics. Following are examples of different bass parts. (Fig. 4-18A-C)

The first example is one in which only notes are written. Notice that it contains mostly quarter notes and is a mixture of both chordal and scalular lines. At letter "C," the bass emphasizes the rhythmic pattern of the entire ensemble, reverting back to the quarter note line thereafter.

Figure 4-18a. "Basie Straight Ahead" by Sammy Nestico, recorded by Count Basie and his Orchestra on the album *Basie Straight Ahead*, Dot DLP 25902. Copyright 1968 by Banes Music, Inc., Kendor Music, Inc., sole selling agent.

The next example combines written notes and chord symbols. The written notes should be played as written as they are an integral part of an

entire ensemble line, improvising the bass line only where chord symbols
appear.

Figure 4–18b. "Warning! Success May Be Hazardous to Your Health" by Toshiko
Akiyoshi, recorded by the Toshiko Akiyoshi-Lew Tabackin Big Band on the album
Road Time, RCA #CPL2-2242. Copyright 1977 by Toba Publishing Company, dis-
tributed by Kendor Music, Inc.

The last example is that of a written "rock" bass line. Notice the more complex rhythms and angularity of this line.

Figure 4-18c. "Goober's New Dune Boogey" by Henry Wolking, measures A¹—B (bass part). Copyright 1975 by Southern Music Company, San Antonio, Texas 78292. Used by permission.

Other things to be considered by the bass player include those aspects relating to the actual sound of the bass—tone and volume. In most instances, the bass should strive for as much sustain as possible, reserving the stopped or short staccato sound for special effects. In order to achieve the best sustaining, the bass player must press the strings to the fingerboard firmly with the left hand. Left-handed players should use their right hand. The actual tone itself can be adjusted by several means. On the bass itself, both acoustic and electric, the place where the string is plucked or picked can make a difference. Playing toward the tail will produce more of a treble sound while playing further up, toward the fingerboard, will produce more of a bass sound. The electric bass will usually have a tone control on it for another means of adjusting the tone. Another place for tone adjustment for the amplified acoustic and electric bass is the control found on the amplifier being used.

Generally speaking, fast tunes will use a little more treble than slower tunes. Whatever the case, make sure the bass line has clarity and definition to it. It may be that a little more treble will have to be added to achieve this. One of the biggest mistakes made by inexperienced players is that their tone has too much bass to it which muddies the sound not only of the bass line itself, but the entire ensemble. Strings also play an important role in the sound of the bass. Round-wound strings will have a little more "bite" to the sound than flat-wound strings, although they are a little more physically taxing to the fingers.

The volume a bass is played at is very crucial. Jazz tunes and ballads will not be played as loudly as rock tunes. Players themselves are not in as good a position to balance volume as the director because they are usually too close to their amps and cannot hear the balance of the ensemble as well as the director. Different amps also have varying acoustic projection properties and it is up to the director to aid the bass player in establishing the proper volume for good balance.

Unlike the other members of the rhythm section, the piano does not have **PIANO** as one of its primary functions that of keeping time. However, that does not preclude that at times the piano player will add to the pulse-keeping of the music.

Piano players in jazz/rock ensembles must think more percussively and rhythmically than what any previous classical training has taught them. In playing behind an ensemble, the pianist should emphasize chord changes and punctuate rhythmic aspects of the ensemble, being careful not to be too "busy" and overplay. Harmonically, the piano player takes on a less important role with the ensemble than when comping (improvised accompanying) behind a soloist. The pianist can often listen to the drummer and adapt many of the rhythmic figures played by the drummer into his or her own part.

Like other members of the rhythm section, the pianist will see different kinds of written parts. Some parts will have everything written out from chord voicings to solos; others may only supply chord symbols. Some may use chord symbols along with exact rhythmic notation. Or, any combination of all the above may be true. The part may be written on a double or single line staff. Occasionally, a bass line will be written into the piano part, most often in charts for younger bands. In such a case, the pianist should not play the bass line unless there is no bass player. If there is no bass player, the pianist must gain the knowledge necessary to developing a good bass line. (See the section covering the bass in this chapter.) There are several key-bass units on the market that operate through amplifiers and can provide a relatively decent sounding bass line when played right.

Following are some examples of piano parts. (Fig. 4-19A-D)

In the first example, two staves are used for the piano part. The bottom line contains the chords to be played with some indications of certain desired rhythmic figures. Also, in the second ending, written notes are included and should be played as written. The top line is written to show piano players what the ensemble is playing so that they may punctuate the rhythmic figures as they see fit.

The next example has everything written out for the pianist plus the inclusion of chord symbols should the piano player choose to use some different voicings. This part most likely should be played as nearly close to the written part as possible though.

The third example includes written chords and pulse marks (slashes) plus the bass line. This is a case in which the bass line would be played by the pianist only in the absence of a bass player.

Figure 4-19a. "Magic Flea" by Sammy Nestico, recorded by Count Basie and his Orchestra on the album *Basie Straight Ahead*, Dot DLP 25902, measures K–L. Copyright 1968 by Banes Music, Inc., Kendor Music, Inc., sole selling agent.

The last example contains three different methods of notation. At the top, the exact voicings desired are written out. At measure 1, the pianist is given the liberty to improvise. At 161, certain rhythmic figures are marked along with pulse marks in order to punctuate ensemble rhythmic figures.

It should be mentioned that the slash marks found in the parts are merely indications of the pulse and very rarely would the pianist play the literal quarter-note chords per pulse.

Figure 4–19b. "Basie Straight Ahead" by Sammy Nestico, recorded by Count Basie and his Orchestra on the album *Basie Straight Ahead*, Dot DLP 25902. Copyright 1968 by Banes Music, Inc., Kendor Music, Inc., sole selling agent.

Figure 4–19c. "Back Home" by Sammy Nestico, measures 1–4 (piano). Copyright 1961 by Kendor Music, Inc.

In up-tempo charts, or charts having many successive chord changes, it is not necessary to play every chord that has been written. To a large extent, it depends on the frequency of the chord changes. If the chords are changing more than twice per bar, most often the concentration should be toward playing those chords falling on the strong beats (1 and 3). Chords that change twice in a bar can generally be played with no problems. If a single chord lasts through one or more bars, it can be repeated using a simple rhythmic pattern and possibly changing the voicing of the chord for added interest. (Voicing will be discussed a little later in this section.) The pianist should eliminate, or at least limit, the use of the pedal so that a more percussive effect can be achieved without running the sound together.

In playing ballads, almost all chords should be played to maintain a continuity of flow throughout the piece. The chords should be played where written, using the pedal to produce smooth change of chords. An occasional rhythmic alteration is acceptable if done in good taste and if it does not create any distraction from the chart. A chord that lasts through one or more measures can be repeated, avoiding rhythmic values of the same duration. Also, a change in voicing could help to prevent any monotony of sound. A chord that lasts only two beats usually should not be repeated. Chords of long duration can be arpeggiated at times, being careful not to overuse this effect.

Whatever style of music is being played and whether the pianist is playing chordal backgrounds or single-line solos, the piano player must articulate the keyboard in the same manner that a horn player articulates the horn. It would be a great asset to the pianist or any other member of the rhythm section to learn the basic "rules" of articulation and phonetics so that they can mentally think out those articulations while playing their instrument. (See Chapter 2, "Articulations.")

Another function of the pianist, not yet mentioned, is to play fills in some of the "holes" in an arrangement. Like the drummer, fills should not be too intricate. They will generally be played in the upper register. The drummer may or may not be filling these same holes. It is possible for both

Figure 4–19d. "Warning! Success May Be Hazardous to Your Health" by Toshiko Akiyoshi, recorded by the Toshiko Akiyoshi-Lew Tabackin Big Band on the album *Road Time*, RCA #CPL2-2242. Copyright 1977 by Toba Publishing Company, distributed by Kendor Music, Inc.

the pianist and the drummer to fill at the same time as long as no conflicts arise. If any conflicts do arise, the two players should have some prior agreement as to which player fills certain holes.

The availability of an electric piano can add flexibility to the sound possibilities available to the pianist. Using the electric piano on the rock charts, some Latin charts, and some of the more contemporary jazz charts can be a refreshing change as well as more appropriate stylistically. The acoustic piano should still be used for most jazz charts and ballads.

Chord voicings were mentioned a little earlier in this chapter. A voicing is the arrangement or position of notes within a chord. There are several things a pianist must know and do to achieve good sounding voicings and smooth voice leading (movement of notes to other notes).

The best sounding voicings generally have the largest intervals at the bottom of the chord with closer spacing near the top. In spacing the notes at the bottom of the chord, stick mainly with the principle notes of that chord. Following are some simple voicings based on the roots of chords using the principle notes as the foundation intervals (Fig. 4-20):

Figure 4-20

Note: A 10th is the third of a chord an octave higher.

Because most ensembles will have a bass, the pianist will most often not use voicings based on chord roots, but will use voicings based on inversions (when a chord's root is not placed at the bottom).

Chord voicings are virtually limitless and it would be impossible to illustrate all the possibilities. An excellent book for acquiring a good foundation in voicing principles and their applications is *Jazz/Rock Voicings for the Contemporary Keyboard Player* by Dan Haerle.[1]

[1] Lebanon, IN: Studio P/R, Inc., 1974.

These are some general suggestions for voicings and their application:

1.   Space the chord tones so that the intervals will be wider at the bottom and closer at the top.

2.   Use primary chord tones as the lowest interval.

3.   Use more rootless voicings when working with a bass.

4.   Avoid wide leaps in moving from chord to chord. Individual chord tones should move as smoothly as possible to a note in the next chord (stepwise).

5.   When possible, maintain common tones, especially on top.

6.   In two-handed voicings, avoid right-hand duplication of the left-hand voicing.

7.   Most voicings that sound good on acoustic piano will also work well on the electric piano. However, it may sometimes be necessary to thin out a particular voicing for clarity because of certain amplification characteristics.

8.   Use a variety of voicings: (a) different inversions; (b) fewer chord tones in softer passages; and (c) more chord tones in heavier passages.

GUITAR

The guitarist has a similar function to that of the pianist in an ensemble situation: to add rhythmic and harmonic aspects to the pulse of a chart. However, the guitarist will be concerned more with steady time playing than the pianist.

In swing-style playing, the guitarist has two basic approaches. One is the most common and is the manner in which Freddie Green of the Count Basie Orchestra is famous for. Short quarter-note chords are played directly on the beat and are played as block chords, not arpeggiated. The second approach has more freedom of rhythm, as in the manner in which a piano part is played. This method allows for different rhythmic patterns, using rests and breaks as a part of the patterns. This latter method can be used in the absence of a piano part, or carefully, to complement the piano part without conflicting with it in any manner.

When playing in the rock style, the guitarist can take more freedom in establishing rhythmic patterns and varying the background from time to time.

No matter what the style, rhythmic clarity is a must so that the sound does not get muddied and run together. To achieve this, just as the bassist does for clarity, the guitarist must also use very firm pressure in holding the strings to the fingerboard. To produce the metronomic strokes per beat, a quick release of the strings is necessary to prevent too much sustaining and running together of beats. This has been called by some the "chunk" method of playing rhythm guitar.

Figure 4-21

A variation of the style of playing quarter notes is to imitate the drummer's basic ride beat. (Fig. 4-21)

Guitar parts are written in a way similar to that of the more advanced piano charts, using a single staff containing mostly chord symbols. Very often, the guitarist and pianist will read from the same part, in which case, certain distinctions should be made as to when the guitar or piano plays alone. These may already be written into the part.

Sometimes notes are written out chordally. This usually is because that particular voicing is desired by the composer or arranger. Sometimes chords with only the top notes are written, and at times, single-line notes appear as part of an ensemble line or written solo. In addition to the pulse marks, which are indicated by slashes, an occasional rhythmic figure is included. It should be played exactly as written as it most likely is emphasizing another section or ensemble figure.

Following are examples of guitar parts. (Figs. 4-22A and 4-22B)

The first example is the most commonly found method of notation used for rhythm guitar parts. This uses chord symbols above the measures containing slash marks indicating that straight time is to be played. At letter "C" and at the fifth bar following it, specific rhythmic figures are indicated and should be played exactly as written, reverting back to time playing where the slash marks appear.

Figure 4–22a. "Basie Straight Ahead" by Sammy Nestico, recorded by Count Basie and his Orchestra on the album *Basie Straight Ahead*, Dot DLP 25902. Copyright 1968 by Banes Music, Inc., Kendor Music, Inc., sole selling agent.

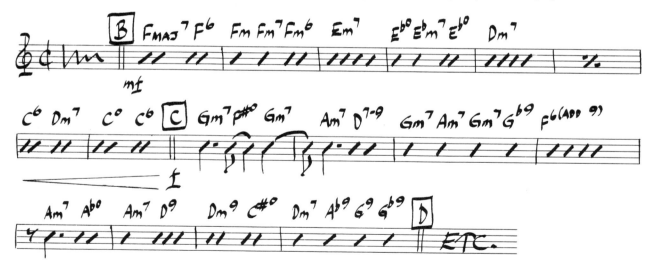

The next example is one in which the guitar has taken on roles other than playing time. At measure 23, the guitar plays a single-line solo in unison with a trumpet. At measure 54, the guitarist is asked to comp with special effects. At measure 64, the part calls for a two-note unison solo line with the piano.

Figure 4-22b. "The Suncatchers" by Marius Nordal. Copyright 1974 by C.L. Barnhouse Co., Oskaloosa, Iowa 52577.

Chord voicing for rhythm guitar should strive for simplicity and smooth voice-leading just as the pianist does. Most often when a complex chord appears in a guitar part, it is a good bet that those harmonies are found somewhere throughout the ensemble, lessening the need for all notes to be present in that chord. Since the main purpose of a rhythm guitar player is to keep time, simplifying the chords by occasionally omitting chord fifths, ninths, elevenths, and thirteenths generally should not take any noticeable effect on the ensemble. This simplification of chords can facilitate smoother voice-leading by not having to move quite so many fingers over large distances. Simple finger shifts and slidings can result in left hand ease of movement. In voicing a chord, the guitarist should listen to and try to complement what the piano player is doing.

Because of the piano being more involved with comping than the guitar, the guitarist must listen to the pianist and, for the most part, play straight time. This is especially during piano solos, when the piano player is probably doing quite a bit of left-hand comping. It is sometimes a good idea for the guitar to lay out during these times to avoid any major conflicts of sound and rhythmic pulse.

The sound (tone and volume) of the guitar will vary depending on the style of chart being played. For the ideal jazz sound, an acoustic instrument with its own amplification system is best (such as the system Freddie Green uses). If a guitar such as this is not available, a regular electric guitar can be used. In such a case, set the controls to get as close to the sound of the first instrument mentioned. For rock charts, a solid body electric guitar is best suited. More treble and volume can be used than with jazz charts. Always be careful not to overpower the ensemble.

The volume of rhythm guitar in the jazz context should be just enough to be "felt" rather than distinctly heard. Whatever the style of music being played, blending the tone and volume characteristically is a very crucial matter for the guitarist to acquire.

THE RHYTHM SECTION AS A UNIT

Chord Symbol Notation

Because rhythm charts contain a great deal of chord symbology, it is a must that the guitarist, bassist, and pianist become familiar with chord construction and symbology. Chord symbology has never been standardized, thus requiring the rhythm player to be aware of the many different ways in which one chord can be symbolized. An illustration of this point comes from Brandt and Roemer's *Standardized Chord Symbol Notation*.[2] (Fig. 4-23)

Figure 4-23

[Fma7]		MAJOR SEVENTH			
F7	FΔ	FΔ7	F♮7	F7♮	F(#7)
F7#	F(7#)	F7+	F(+7)	Fm7	FM7
FM7	Fma	FMaj7	Fma7	Fmj7	Fma7
Fmaj7	F7ma	FMaj7	FMJ7	Fma7	Fm7

Standardized Chord Symbol Notation is an excellent reference in learning the many different variants of notation. It is also a good source method for arriving at a uniform system of notation that is clearly indicative of the chord to be played.

[2] Carl Brandt and Clinton Roemer, *Standardized Chord Symbol Notation*, 2nd ed. (Sherman Oaks, CA: Roerick Music Co., 1976), p. 7.

Backgrounds

The purpose of the rhythm section collectively is to provide the rhythmic and harmonic basis of an ensemble. Each member contributes his or her individual efforts, as previously discussed, to achieve a unified, solid sectional sound.

When playing with an ensemble, the rhythm section is somewhat, though not entirely, restricted to the basic function of rhythm and harmony. However, when the time comes to provide a background for a soloist, the section's role alters to that not only of support, but takes on one of influence and instigation. Rhythms, harmonies, and textures all serve as a means of creating interest and excitement in working with a soloist. Not only can the rhythm section feed off of various melodic, harmonic, and rhythmic aspects of a solo, but it can also provide ideas in those same areas for the soloist to use, as long as the section does not influence the soloist to the extent that he or she is completely controlled.

Background *rhythms* can affect the motion of a solo. For instance, a slow moving, sustained background can enhance a solo of long phrases in a ballad setting, or it can act as a stabilizer of time behind a solo containing much rhythmic complexity. A fast moving background can add energy to a solo that is using longer, sustained notes, or it can intensify the energy of an already fast moving solo.

Harmony can add coloration and movement to a solo. In playing behind a lyrical solo, simple triads with a few added sevenths, ninths, and so forth enhance the lyricism without creating unwanted tension. By adding more chord tones and alterations of chord tones, more tension is created toward prompting more motion in the solo lines. Chord changes under repeated or sustained melodic notes will help the feeling of motion and interest.

Textures are something else to be considered in building a background. Heavy block-chording can act as a rhythmic stabilizer as well as create a feel of heaviness. Arpeggiating the chords will thin out the texture, keep rhythmic stability, and complement a lighter melodic line. Melodic and octave doubling can change the character of a solo as well as the playing of a countermelody. Another effective textural device, if not used too much, is to drop all background for a while. Or, have only the drums or bass playing with the soloist, eventually adding each member of the rhythm section.

Whatever texture or style of background being used, keep in mind the balance of accompaniment to the soloist. Flutes and vibes, for instance, are much softer by nature and must be dealt with accordingly. The use of solo microphones through a P.A. system can aid greatly in overcoming balance problems. The taste and discretion of backgrounds is built on experience. Experiment with all aspects and develop a good inner sense for backgrounds.

Special Devices

Available to all the members of the rhythm section are a wide variety of special devices for sound alteration. The guitar and electric piano are the most likely to use these sound alteration devices. Such things include wah-wah pedals, fuzz-boxes, phase shifters, and a multitude of others too numerous to list. New devices are being invented constantly. The electric bass will occasionally use some of these, although not to the extent the guitar and electric piano do. Drums too can alter their sound through the use of electronic transducers.

In using these special devices, care must be taken not to overuse them. This would result in the loss of impact and effect. Also, it is still important to maintain a good balance with the rest of the ensemble.

Listen to the Pros

Perhaps the best teacher available to any player is sound recordings. It is particularly important that the members of any rhythm section listen to what the pros are doing in all types of settings. Remember that the rhythm section will work in many contexts: ensemble, section, and solo. It is important that they know and execute proper approaches to each situation. Listen to what is being done behind ensemble or section passages, behind soloists, and when the rhythm section is working by itself. Any listening is bound to result in improved concept and actual performance.

Rehearsal Techniques 5

The quality and success of any organization's performance is greatly determined by what takes place throughout the rehearsal sequence. This especially holds true for younger, less experienced groups.

Through a basically systematic approach toward rehearsal, gratifying results will come with much greater ease than with some haphazard approach. Following are some suggestions that can be used, or portions incorporated into a rehearsal routine. Careful evaluation and re-evaluation of approach must be a part of this rehearsal sequence in order to prevent stagnation anywhere within the overall program.

PLANNING

Planning is an area too often overlooked when approaching a rehearsal. Good planning leads to a more productive rehearsal and less wasted time. Productive planning rests on the director and/or section leaders during out-of-rehearsal time, defining certain goals and accomplishments, and a means of achieving them.

Study scores thoroughly, perhaps along with a recording if it is available, or with one of your own rehearsal tapes. You can get ideas from the recordings as well as original ideas injected into the preparation of the score (with regard to phrasings, articulations, tempos, dynamics, attacks and releases, and special effects and interpretations). Be sure to mark down all your thoughts regarding the above so that it is possible to talk through the chart with the ensemble or section. (Use a pencil so that changes, if necessary, can be easily made.)

Mapping out the time to be spent on certain areas needs to be somewhat flexible, yet adhere to some sort of rigidity. Be sure to include some time for a rest or break, especially when working on a very taxing piece of music. If the total time allotment is somewhat limited, this could be, in part, accomplished by mixing the style of tunes to be rehearsed. For instance, interject an easy-blowing ballad between other harder-blowing tunes. Another suggestion might be to work on sectional or solo areas for awhile, allowing the others time to rest.

Other areas of value that can be planned into a rehearsal sequence is time to listen to professional recordings of charts in the book, and time to listen to the group through the use of rehearsal tapes. Another extremely important area is sight reading. This is an area greatly overlooked and can be of tremendous value to a program.

Always plan to be open to the suggestions of ensemble members. There is much imagination and creativity in many of the players that can add greatly to the ensemble. Above all, have confidence in the goals you've set and what you are doing. Do not always take an overly serious approach toward achieving these goals. A relaxed, yet structured, atmosphere will yield the greatest results.

ENSEMBLE   Before the actual rehearsal begins, each player should have spent an adequate amount of time warming up and getting some close relative tuning done. Tuning is a must before any rehearsing is started. Periodic spot checks on tuning should be made throughout the course of a rehearsal. (Tuning and intonation have already been discussed in Chapter 1.)

The director should discuss briefly what he or she intends to rehearse and what he or she hopes the ensemble will accomplish. This gives a sort of "mini-goal" toward which to work. *Part marking* is a must during rehearsal time. Before rehearsing a chart, the director should have a "talk-through" with the ensemble, making sure they have marked their parts in the same manner as the score. You can avoid many problems and save a lot of time by doing this. Make sure the marking is done with pencil only so that changes can be made.

Several things that could be marked in the parts include:

1.   Phrase markings (⌒)

2.   Special articulation markings (See Chapter 2 and Appendix A.)

3.   Line contouring (See Chapter 3.)

4. Releases (Use a minus sign: –2, –2½, and so on.) Also indicate when there is to be a tongue release. (See Chapter 2.)

5. Special effects (See Chapter 2 and Appendix A.)

6. Dynamic markings (See Chapter 1.) Circle the most important and those that are in sharp contrast to the previous one.

7. Line dominance (See Chapter 1.)

Once the parts have been marked, then a "play-through" from top to bottom is in order. This will give the ensemble a general concept of the desired styling of the chart. If a recording is available, play it for the ensemble and have them watch their music, marking notes as to interpretation.

The subject of *listening* can be a very important factor in developing good jazz concepts. More and more, recordings of charts are becoming available through the publishers, college recordings, and recordings by professionals themselves. A few of these professionals with recordings of published charts include Woody Herman, Thad Jones/Mel Lewis, Stan Kenton, Maynard Ferguson, and Toshiko Akiyoshi/Lew Tabackin.

It is very important to make the players aware of what they are listening for, such as listed in the things to be marked in the parts. The rhythm section should pay particular attention to what is being played, as most rhythm charts are very sketchy regarding fills, punctuations, and so on. After listening to a recorded chart, have the ensemble read it down, trying to sound as much like the professionals as possible. Keep in mind that it is not wrong to use a different interpretation. Imitation is a starting point from which to develop original styles.

It would be advantageous to keep a master tape of the charts the group is working on from which each member would be able to make their own tapes for individual study and practice. Taping a rehearsal regularly for critical evaluation by the director and the ensemble is also a great rehearsal tool.

In working with a chart that is fairly new to the group, it might help at some point to have just the lead players, plus rhythm, play their parts until they have grasped the desired "feel" of the chart. Then start adding the inner parts until the entire group is phrasing and playing in the same manner as the lead players.

Various *seating arrangements* can be used for the ensemble. The manner in which a band sets up can be dictated by personal preference, available space, desired sound dispersion, or many other factors. There are three basic seating arrangements that the majority of ensembles use for performance.

The most widely used and probably the best arrangement conducive to a tight, controlled situation is the "stack." In the stack arrangement, the saxes are in front; trombones are directly behind; the trumpets are in the rear; and the rhythm is to one side. (Fig. 5-1)

Figure 5-1

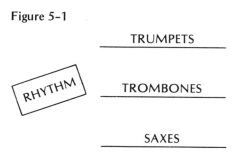

Preferably, the saxes will be sitting on the floor; the trombones sitting on a short riser behind the saxes; and the trumpets standing on a riser the same height as the trombones are sitting on. The rhythm section could set up on the floor, on risers, or a mixture. This use of risers allows each section to project without blowing into the person in front of them, which would result in less projection.

If the brass overpowers the reeds, you may choose to do away with the use of risers for the brass. Another, more preferable alternative, is to use presence microphones on the saxes. Try to avoid any playing into the stands other than for special effects. Have the stands low enough or off to one side so as not to block any sound. This also serves to avoid any alteration of tone quality.

Another popular seating arrangement is the "spread" formation, which puts the rhythm section in the center at the rear, the saxes on one side, and the brass on the other. (Fig. 5-2)

Figure 5-2

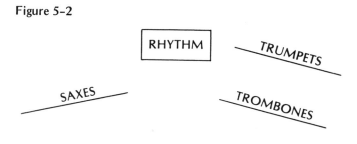

The angle at which the horns sit can be varied from a basically open to a closed situation. This method of seating will produce a sound that is not quite as focused—straight ahead and direct—as the first, and sometimes will create problems in precision of the ensemble.

The third seating arrangement is the type the Stan Kenton Orchestra used. It is called the "horseshoe" set-up. Here, the horns surround the centrally located rhythm section. (Fig. 5-3)

Figure 5–3

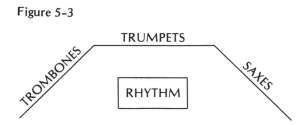

Within the ensemble itself, no matter which set-up is used, certain guidelines of individual seating can be followed to produce the best sound while achieving precision.

1. Lead players should be at the center of each section.

2. The "jazz chairs" (soloists) should be as close to the rhythm section as possible.

3. The tenor saxes should be placed at either side of the alto saxes.

4. The bass trombone and bari sax should be located on the same side of the band.

5. The rhythm section should be as close to the ensemble as possible.

    a. The bass player should stand slightly to the left and behind the drummer's hi-hat.

    b. The guitar player should be next to the bass.

    c. The piano player should be slightly forward and to the side of the rest of the rhythm section.

For rehearsal purposes, the seating in each section at times can vary so that they may gain more awareness of the other parts. Something else that can be done is to have the saxes facing the brass, allowing the brass players to gain more awareness of the sax parts. A third suggestion would be to sit in a large circle, space permitting. This works very well for sectional rehearsals.

Rehearsal facilities can have an effect on a performance. If the opportunity is present, rehearse in different rooms or facilities so that you do not get used to only one sound. If at all possible, hold at least one rehearsal in the place where there is to be an upcoming performance, preferably on the same day.

Another factor to consider is the use of a P.A. system. If you use a P.A. system for performances, be sure to spend a fair amount of rehearsal time with it. Nothing can spoil a good performance faster than misuse of sound systems. It is also good to get the ensemble, and especially the soloists, used to using microphones and for the rhythm section to be able to better hear the soloists. For the majority of performance situations (except in large open areas) the purpose of a P.A. system should be to help create a balance between sections, striving to keep as close to an acoustic sound as possible. Following is a good method of microphone placement for these purposes. (Fig. 5-4)

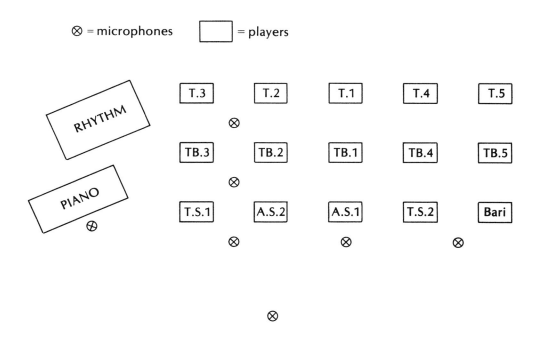

1. Three "presence" microphones for the saxes. These remain "live" (on) throughout the performance at just enough volume to balance the brass. They can also be used for solo purposes.

2. One microphone for the trombone section and one microphone for the trumpet section to be used for solo purposes. These microphones should have an on/off switch and should be live only during solos. If there is more than one soloist at any time from the same section, more microphones could be used under the same circumstances.

3. Several methods are available for miking acoustic pianos. There are a few good transducers (pickups) that can be fed directly into a P.A. system or a separate amplifier. If one is not available, then good microphone placement can help out. On a grand piano, usually only one microphone is needed. Place it as close to one of the tone holes in the metal plate under the lid

as possible without touching the sides. Experiment with moving this microphone around until the most even sound pickup is achieved. Another possibility is the use of a second microphone under the piano, close to the sound board. On an upright style piano, one, or preferably two microphones should be placed close to the sound board from the rear of the piano. Use caution in placing these microphones so as not to be touching anything as feedback or roaring might occur.

4.   Have a microphone out front for announcing and/or soloing.

Whatever your situation, the least amount of microphones and the least usage of a P.A. system, the better. This not only promotes a clearer, more natural sound, but eliminates possible problems that might interfere with a good performance.

The choice of *rehearsal tempos* can be a problem unless care is taken to recognize certain factors. Many of the faster moving technical charts are sometimes played easier at a faster tempo—as they may not lay well for certain instruments and achieve the proper effect if played too slowly. The problem that might arise with rehearsing a fast tempo is that the pulse may be rushed and technical problems may arise. In ballads and slower tempo charts, more liberty can be taken with the tempo. However, do not create a feeling of dragging whatever you do as it could psychologically be detrimental to the players' enthusiasm toward the music. The best thing to do is to experiment with various tempos until you have arrived at a feel that is comfortable for the ensemble and the nature of the music being played.

As mentioned earlier in this chapter, *sight reading* can be an extremely valuable inclusion for a rehearsal sequence. It gives the ensemble a chance to read a lot of different styles and rhythmic figures which can only serve to sharpen their musical abilities and add breadth to their experience in playing. It also creates a freshness in a rehearsal where a lot of hard work and concentration are being spent on working up a series of charts for performance purposes.

You can save valuable time by having separate sight-reading folders previously made up. The folders can be passed out and picked up by librarians, who can also change the music frequently. If your library is somewhat limited, several directions can be pursued in obtaining sight-reading material. Music stores will often let you take new music on approval, in which case you are reading the new music and at the same time, reviewing it for possible purchase for your library. Another way is to borrow charts from other schools or sources. If a talented writer is a member of the ensemble, be sure to include that material as well.

The approach to reading a piece of music is much the same as in the rehearsal procedure for a performance piece. The main difference will be the time spent on each of the points mentioned earlier in this chapter.

A talk through should be done pointing out all the stylistic markings (dynamics, phrases, articulations, and so forth). Stylistic markings are equally important to the notes themselves. Also be aware of any key changes, repeats, endings, D.S.s, D.C.s, and Codas. Take tempos where they are comfortable. A tempo that is too fast defeats the objectives of sight reading. Likewise, a tempo that is too slow doesn't make the most of the objectives. Don't dwell on errors. Keep playing and concentrate on knowing where the beat or pulse is (most importantly, the first beat of every measure.) Of course, it might be necessary to stop in the middle of a piece, due to some disastrous errors, and regroup the flow of the chart.

Sight reading does not have to be done every day, but some regular scheduling of it will be a great boost to the program.

SECTIONS   Sectional rehearsals can go a long way toward achieving the precision needed for good performances. Intensified concentration on certain aspects of a particular section can help immeasurably, without having to worry about the entire ensemble (though it is still good to keep an awareness of the complete picture).

Section rehearsals can be handled several ways. "Sectionals" could replace an ensemble rehearsal every once in awhile, or preferably be conducted at some other time. At least once or twice per week would be good for sectionals. Various combinations could be run:

1.   Each separate section by itself (saxes, trumpets, trombones, rhythm)

2.   Trumpets and trombones

3.   Brass and rhythm or partial rhythm (bass and drums)

4.   Saxes and rhythm or partial rhythm

5.   Soloists and rhythm

6.   Ensemble without rhythm

Again, variations in seating can help unify precision aspects and possibly clear up problems caused by the lack of awareness of other parts.

Many times, section rehearsals can be handled by the section leaders, which saves the director a lot of time. It is a good idea for the director to be present at least part of the time for each section rehearsal.

These smaller rehearsals allow the sections to work out any technical problems and arrive at exactly the same interpretations of articulation, phrasing, and so on. Again, the parts should always be marked with pencil as they are worked out and decided upon.

It is important that any changes of interpretation be made known to the director and the ensemble so that they can adjust accordingly. The different ideas and experimentation found in sectionals can result in a more creative performance.

A good performance by the ensemble can be marred by the soloists not **SOLOISTS** meeting the level achieved by the ensemble. Soloing, most often improvised soloing, is an area that needs much attention. Before trying to solo, a player must have a working knowledge of the basic needs for improvisation. (See Chapter 7.) A great deal of time must be spent in individual work on the basics of improvisation. When ready to do soloing, different approaches may be taken to work on specific solos.

The most obvious approach is to get together with the rhythm section and work through the solo. This is very necessary in order for the rhythm section to get some idea of what to expect from the soloist, and to get some sort of rapport established. It is sometimes difficult to get the entire rhythm section together for this type of rehearsal because many things are demanded of their time. Specific times should be set up to work live with the rhythm section.

A recorded rhythm section background can aid the soloist in his or her practice. This allows the soloist to practice soloing at his or her convenience, as much as desired. It will also relieve the rhythm section of some of their time spent, as other soloists may want to work on their solos also.

When rehearsing a solo, either with the rhythm section or the taped background, soloists should record themselves frequently to listen, evaluate, and critically analyze what they are doing. It is also a good idea for the director to hear these tapes and offer guidance and suggestions.

If the solo is contained in a chart that has been recorded by an advanced group or professionals, try to obtain the recording and analyze what is being done with the phrasing, articulations, special effects, and dynamics. Then try to imitate some of the outstanding sytlistic characteristics and include them within your own ideas. Imitation can be a great teacher if it is not used exclusively.

Most of all, keep listening. Listen to all types of solos and soloists and begin to gain and develop a good concept of or feel for improvisation.

The end result, the actual performance and subsequent learning, is dictated by the success of previous rehearsals, whether it is the entire ensemble, sectionals, or soloists.

6 Performances

MUSIC SELECTION Music selection is an area of great importance and the responsibility of selection rests primarily upon the director. Care must be taken not to select music that is beyond the technical and physical capabilities of the group. Too often, a young ensemble is prevailed upon by the director to play charts that professionals are playing. This often forces brass players to play beyond their range and volume limits, and reeds to attempt technical passages they cannot cope with.

It is very important that young ensembles first develop a basic understanding of techniques and interpretations of the various styles for performance and to execute them properly. Several method books are available which start with very simple exercises and tunes that can be selected for performance and help develop this understanding.

As the group progresses, more difficult music can be selected containing more complex rhythms, extended ranges, and soloing, progressing from the written solo to the improvised solo.

Some music is written with woodwind doubles. Hopefully, the more advanced sax players will have studied other woodwind instruments so that they may handle these doubles, most usually flute or clarinet and sometimes oboe and bass clarinet. It may be necessary sometimes to bring in extra players to cover these parts if the sax players are not able to double adequately.

Also found is music for augmented ensemble. This could include extra woodwinds, French horns, tuba, percussion, and/or strings. This is usually called a "studio" type instrumentation.

With the rise in popularity of vocal jazz ensembles, more and more music is being written combining the instrumental and vocal ensembles.

Because the selection of music is so important and is often influenced by budget and time restrictions, the following suggestions are offered to help ease the process:

1. Go to music stores and look through scores.

2. Listen to recordings.

    (a) Many publishers have free demonstration recordings.

    (b) Some publishers have reference libraries of recordings available for a very small fee.

    (c) Some published charts have been recorded by the pros and are available on commercial recordings.

3. Attend reading clinics.

4. Attend others' programs, contests, and festivals.

5. Several music publications list and review new music such as the *NAJE Educator,* the *Music Educators Journal,* the *Instrumentalist,* and the *School Musician.*

6. Appendix C contains a list of jazz chart sources. Most of these sources will send complete listings on request. A music store may also have the listings.

Again, remember to select music that is within the capabilities of the group, yet presents challenges. Also, develop a well-rounded library that contains a wide variety of styles.

The music selection for performance is a difficult task to approach. Several factors enter into this, such as time allotment, musical worth balanced with entertainment aspects, variety of styles, charts that bring out the strong points of an ensemble or soloists, and more.

PROGRAMMING

An effective performance is the result of good selection of charts, a good progression of elements (contrasting styles, moods, tempos, keys) and a good sense of production.

Once charts have been selected that are appropriate to the group's abilities and are varied in style and tempo, the director must then arrange them into a sequence that is balanced and helpful to the performers. Even though the members of the ensemble will have "warmed up" before a performance, the first number should be one that the ensemble has extra confidence in playing as they have to adjust to playing before an audience and need to overcome any tension to become relaxed and comfortable with the music and audience. From there on, the element of contrast and moving through light and heavy works takes over.

A program can open in various ways and it is up to the director to decide how he or she wants to program the pieces. One good comparison of programming is with the classical four-movement symphony. Each movement emphasizes something different musically, yet contributes to the overall effect of the entire symphony. An example of this type of programming a jazz set could be the following:

1. Medium-fast swing
2. Ballad
3. Latin or jazz waltz
4. Up-tempo "shouter"

Whatever length of program you have, it should open relatively strong, but not with your most powerful chart. (At contests and festivals, you would probably be duplicating the style of chart last played by the previous band.) The middle number should be in contrast, such as a ballad, and always end up-tempo with your most impressive number.

Other programming ideas could include changing the size of group. Near the middle of a program, a smaller combo could be featured. Toward the end, the ensemble could be expanded by adding French horns, a tuba, extra woodwinds, strings, or a choir. This contraction and expansion of size can be both aurally and visually refreshing to an audience.

Another aspect related to programming is the inclusion of a little showmanship. If not overdone, this can add interest to a program. Perhaps a player could solo from where the audience is seated, or backstage; the entire band could sing unison scat licks. Or, a small combo could stroll through the audience. Keep in mind, not too many of these surprises on one program. At a contest or festival, it is not recommended to try any fancy showmanship devices.

Good soloists should be given as much time as possible to show off their talents. If a soloist is extremely talented, he or she should be given the time to fully develop ideas. Provided the soloist is this talented, the band could leave the stage for a period of time while the soloist performs sort of a "mini-concerto."

For a jazz performance, a relaxed, informal atmosphere is best. Tuxedos are not necessary, nor are uniforms of any type. The director must keep in mind not to overconduct as the band's performance is much more important than the director's flamboyance. Short announcements and introductions of soloists between tunes add to the informal atmosphere and allow the ensemble to relax and rest a bit.

Related to programming is the use of guest artists. Often, a guest artist or artists will come in prior to a performance and clinic the band. Many have charts of differing grades of difficulty that can be performed with the artist on a program. If the program is to be in one segment, the best place to bring in the guest artist is toward the end. If the program is divided into two segments, then bring in the artist at the close of the first segment and again toward the end of the second.

Always start a program on time and avoid an overly long performance. An hour to an hour and fifteen minutes is sufficient if one group is presented; and an hour and a half to an hour and forty-five minutes if more than one group is presented. If the performance is to be more than an hour, an intermission around the half-way mark should be scheduled to allow both the audience and performers to rest. It is better for the audience to leave wishing they could hear more than to have them feel they were subjected to an ordeal, no matter how well the music was played.

CONCERTS

Factors other than actual programming are a great part of giving concerts. The opportunities for performance are wide and varied. The evening concert is the major type of performance. Other opportunities include performing before civic organizations, business meetings, school assemblies, and more.

For whatever type of performance and place, good planning and preparation is a must. Scheduling is probably the most difficult task of planning and preparation. It is wise to plan a performance schedule well in advance, taking into consideration the number of concerts, the extent of involvement in each concert, and the preparation time required of the music. Time between performances should be allowed both for preparation of performance and nonperformance (study-type) music.

Another major factor is planning around other scheduled activities so that audience attendance can be at its maximum. Check community and school activity calendars, sporting events, and other concerts and productions so that little or no conflicts arise. When tentative dates have been decided upon, arrangements should be made to schedule the place of performance, not only for the performance itself, but a dress rehearsal as well.

Lighting and sound equipment must be checked out. Make arrangements to transport stands, chairs, and equipment if necessary. Organize publicity campaigns. Have programs printed if they are to be used, and line up ushers and box office personnel and stage crew. You should also arrange for a tape recorder and a qualified person to run it. All this and more should be taken care of far in advance of the concert.

CONTESTS AND FESTIVALS

The subject of contests and festivals is one of great controversy among music educators. There are strong feelings both pro and con, each side having justifiable statements or arguments.

Although school band contests have been around since approximately 1923 on a national level, the jazz contest did not start until around 1959.

There are two basic types of contests and/or festivals: competitive and noncompetitive. These can range from a one- or two-day event up to a week or longer and be handled in a number of ways.

Competitive contests will rank the groups in order according to their performance, most usually the top three to five groups. Sometimes, classifications are made based on the school's enrollment or number of students in a music program and rankings for each separate class assigned. Often, the top groups in each classification are asked to perform again and are then ranked overall.

The noncompetitive format is one in which no ratings or rankings are given, but one in which groups participate merely for critique.

Between those two extremes is the concept of rating a performance against a pre-set standard and numerical ratings assigned. This allows more than one band to receive a top rating and leaves the comparisons and conclusions to the directors and participants.

Criticisms can be written, taped, or both. The use of taping is becoming increasingly popular as criticisms can be pinpointed to the exact spot in the music as it is being recorded. This can save an adjudicator much time trying to write everything down, plus enable a director or ensemble to more clearly understand what is meant by a certain criticism.

Some festivals or contests may select an "all-star" band that may rehearse a short while and perform later on in a concert. The use of performer/adjudicators with top bands is also very popular. Clinics given by these artists can be an invaluable experience for participants in a contest or festival of this sort.

The main reasons for the shift toward the noncompetitive end of the scale are directed at educational values versus arbitrary competitive elements. A major criticism of competitive situations is that it overstresses the element of winning to the extent that too much time is spent working on contest numbers, ignoring the educational attributes of covering more and varied literature.

One of the things that can aid in preventing such a situation is the inclusion of sight-reading at a contest. This to some extent will force directors to focus a little more attention to the reading aspect rather than just to total preparation of a few numbers.

A good contest or festival is one in which several of the following are included in addition to the performances of the groups:

1. Clinics on improvisation

2. Individual instruction on the separate instruments and/or sections

3. Arranging and rehearsal techniques

4. Displays

5. Jam sessions

6. Rap sessions

In an effort to improve the quality and educational value of jazz festivals and contests, the National Association of Jazz Educators (NAJE) has developed a set of guidelines, both mandatory and suggested, in order to become an "NAJE-Approved" festival. Following are the guidelines (Fig. 6-1) and the NAJE Adjudication Form (Fig. 6-2).

Whether in rehearsal, performing a concert, or participating in a contest or festival, it is extremely important to keep in touch with truly educational goals and not let the "spirit of competition" rule your approach to jazz and its related elements.

NAJE "APPROVED FESTIVAL" APPLICATION

In an effort to improve the quality of jazz festivals across the country, the National Association of Jazz Educators has developed the following mandatory guidelines. Please examine these rules carefully, fill in the appropriate areas, sign, and return to NAJE Festivals Chairman, Box 724, Manhattan, Ks. 66502.

MANDATORY GUIDELINES

_____ A MINIMUM OF THREE QUALIFIED JUDGES.

_____ SIGHT READING (usually requires a fourth judge.) Including the sight reading score, if competitive, is not mandatory the first year.

_____ USE OF THE OFFICIAL NAJE JAZZ ADJUDICATION FORM.

_____ USE OF NAJE TALENT CITATIONS.

_____ SUFFICIENT STAGE LIGHTING, SATISFACTORY ACOUSTICS, RISERS, GOOD QUALITY P.A. SYSTEM, MUSIC STANDS, ETC.

_____ GOOD QUALITY PIANO TUNED TO 440.

_____ CONSISTENT SCHEDULING OF GROUPS BY CLASSIFICATION.

_____ SOME MEANS OF COMMUNICATION BETWEEN THE JUDGES AND THE STAGE AREA.

_____ A SEATING PLAT OF EACH GROUP SHOWING NAMES, INSTRUMENT (OR PART), AND YEAR IN SCHOOL.

_____ A DETERMINATION OF THE GROUP'S ELIGIBILITY TO RECEIVE NAJE TALENT CITATIONS/SCHOLARSHIPS. (Director must be a member of NAJE for group to be eligible. Judges should be notified of director's status.)

_____ CLEAR AND CONCISE RULES, REGULATIONS AND OTHER INFORMATION TO PARTICI-PANTS WELL IN ADVANCE OF PERFORMANCE.

_____ VERIFICATION TO THE JUDGES THAT EACH STUDENT IS ELIGIBLE TO PERFORM WITH THE GROUP.

_____ SCORES FOR THE JUDGES.

I have read the above rules for an NAJE "Approved Festival" and have indicated with a check the items that will be incorporated into my festival. I confirm with my signature that the above is true.

_____   _____
(name of festival)   Festival Director (sign)

_____   _____
(festival location)   Festival Director (PRINT NAME)

_____
(city)   (state)   (zip) (phone)   (festival dates)

_____
(judge's name – address)

_____
(judge's name – address)

_____
(judge's name – address)

_____
(judge's name – address)

(Put a check by judge's name if he is not a member of NAJE.)

This is the _____ year for the festival   Date: _____

National Association of Jazz Educators, Box 724, Manhattan, Ks 66502

Figure 6-1. Used by permission.

Jazz Performance

Prepared by the National Association of Jazz Educators

RATING

Use no plus or minus signs in final rating

Event ______________________ Class ________ Date ____________19____

Name of Organization ______________________ No. of Players ________

School ______________________ Director ______________________

City ____________ State ________ District ________ School Enrollment ________

COMMENTS

Use reverse side for additional comments

ENSEMBLE 45 Points Total	
Overall Tonal Texture	
Authority & Precision	
Time and Interpretation	
Total Points	

Rhythm Section 35 Points Total	
Balance	
Fills and Band Back-up	
Time and Rhythmic Feel	
Total Points	

SOLOS/IMPROVISATION 20 Points Total	
Woodwinds	
Brass	
Rhythm	
Total Points	

GRAND TOTAL	

Recommended Division Rating Criteria: 85 and above - I, 70-84 - II, below 70 - III. The numerical system is intended to serve as a guide for final classification and should not replace common sense and good judgment.

____
Adjudicator

Adjudicator's private comments for ______________________ (Name of Director)**, to be detached by *adjudicator* and sealed in attached envelope furnished by Festival Chairman.**

Choice of materials ____
Program order ____
Stage presence
and communication ____
Other __________ ____

Rating Criteria
A - Excellent
B - Good
C - Fair
D - Poor

Use reverse side for additional comments

Figure 6-2. Copyright 1978 by National Association of Jazz Educators.

ENSEMBLE TEXTURE

This term is intended to include Balance, Blend, Intonation, Quality of Sound, and other intangibles which contribute to the overall sound of the Ensemble. It should be recognized that a band can be perfectly in tune, have a good blend, and be perfectly balanced and still have a mediocre sound because of thin tones, strident quality, unsupported pitches, etc. It is felt that the adjudicator would evaluate the general ensemble sound and comment on any weakness that affects the total sound.

AUTHORITY AND PRECISION

These terms have to do with the manner in which phrases are attacked and released. Good bands play with complete confidence and are very precise in the beginning and ending of phrases, dynamics, nuances, etc.

TIME AND INTERPRETATION

The term TIME refers to the manner in which rhythmic patterns are played within the phrase. The notes must be stylistically accurate. Interpretation also refers to the musically sensitive interpretation of the various jazz styles.

BALANCE

Rhythm sections should be balanced within themselves and in terms of the Ensemble.

FILLS & BAND BACK-UP

The fills used should be appropriate to the musical style and the band back-up refers to rhythmic awareness and support of the Ensemble phrases.

TIME & RHYTHMIC FEEL

The Rhythm Section must provide the basic pulsation for the Ensemble. The patterns played should be an effort by the total rhythm section and should be balanced or structured to support the Ensemble.

SOLOS & IMPROVISATION

Solos can be learned and played, or improvisation can be elected. In either case, the performance should be in keeping with the style of the selection and should enhance the general performance at that point.

Prepared by the National Association of Jazz Educators

(Private comments continued)

Signature of Adjudicator _____

Basic Needs
for Improvisation 7

Jazz improvisation is a multi-faceted subject, and it would be impossible to comprehensively cover all areas in a single book, much less a single chapter. The intention of this chapter is to provide an awareness of the *basic* needs for improvisation and to act as a reference springboard toward methods and materials that serve as study aids in the practice of this art.

Many excellent sources are available to the student of improvisation, and some will be referred to throughout the course of this chapter. In addition, others not mentioned specifically within are listed in Appendix C, hopefully to provide further reference. It is impossible to recommend only a few as being the best or most important and/or comprehensive.

Improvisation has often been labeled as spontaneous, creative, and innovative composition or creation. This is not entirely true. The majority of improvisation, as we know it, has been built on a long line of developmental processes, including the elementary studying of scales, patterns, motifs, listening to others and imitating those ideas. The creativity part comes in with the manner in which all these contributing factors are melded together to form the improvised solo.

These factors will be dealt with in this chapter. In the past, many people felt that improvisation could not be "taught" in the traditional sense of teaching. A few people still feel this way today. Those people believed the only way to learn was by "doing," through jam sessions and the like. It often took years to develop, by trial and error, the same skills most people today are learning in a relatively short period of time through the use of current teaching methods and aids. The technical aspects can be taught to virtually anyone who tries. The factors that separate the good improviser from the mediocre are those that are abstract and intangible, such as personality factors, physical agility, intelligence, emotional levels, and intuition.

The elements comprising the study of improvisation, although actually intertwined, can be broken into several general categories. Following are short discussions of these.

PRE-STUDY   Before undertaking the study of improvisation, a certain level of competency in basic instrumental disciplines such as fingerings, sound production, intonation, embouchure development, breathing, and technique should already be accomplished. These disciplines should be on such a level that the student of improvisation does not have to stop and worry about them at the same time he or she is trying to take in all the factors related to improvisational development. The improviser should also be able to play a written solo of medium difficulty. While reading is not absolutely necessary for learning to improvise, it greatly facilitates and speeds up the process, as much of the matter for study that follows can be found in many method books for practice purposes.

SCALES, CHORDS, AND INTERVALS   The student must learn and practice many different scales and chords. The understanding of how scales and chords are built in itself is not enough. The facility with which they are played is extremely important. The scales used in jazz include all common major, minor, and modal scales, as well as some more exotic scales. For the beginning improviser, the major, minor, and modal scales should be learned in *all* keys, from the lowest note on the instrument to the highest note within his or her comfortable range. These should be practiced in as many ways as can be thought of. Following are some suggestions:

> 1.   Ascend and descend on scales built on the roots moving clockwise around the cycle of keys (circle of fifths): C, F, B-flat, E-flat, and so on. (Fig. 7-1)
>
> 2.   Reverse the order, moving counterclockwise: C, G, D, A, and so on.
>
> 3.   Practice scales based on roots a whole step apart: C, D, E, and so on.
>
> 4.   Practice scales based on roots a half-step apart, in chromatic order: C, C-sharp, D, E-flat, and so on.
>
> 5.   Practice scales using a variety of rhythms, articulations, and dynamics.

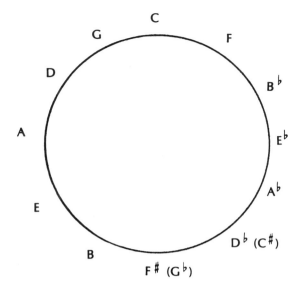

Figure 7-1

Most books on improvisation will include sections devoted to scale technique development. An excellent practice method for scales is *Scales for Jazz Improvisation* by Dan Haerle.[1]

Corresponding with the study and practice of scales is that of chords and their make-up. Early studies should include basic chord-running (arpeggios) on major and minor triads and seventh chords in all keys. Eventually, practice should also include the use of chord extensions, diminished chords, augmented chords, compound chords, chords with altered functions, suspensions, and polytonal chords.

It is necessary for the improviser to be familiar with the make-up of chords and their corresponding symbology. Probably the best reference for the basic construction and symbology of chords is Brandt and Roemer's *Standardized Chord Symbol Notation,*[2] which is also an excellent source of the many different varieties of chord symbology being used by the many arrangers and composers. Chords can be practiced in a similar manner as the scales were—around the circle of fifths, scale-wise, chromatically, using variations of style.

The student should also have a knowledge of intervals in addition to those comprising chords, such as fourths, fifths, diminished fifths, sixths, major and minor sevenths, ninths, elevenths, raised elevenths, thirteenths, and so on. In other words, *all* intervals.

PATTERNS

Once a basic understanding of the construction of scales and chords and their symbology has been accomplished, the improviser should look toward finding ways of realizing the chord symbols through playing in a more interesting, imaginative, and economical manner. Not all notes

[1] Dan Haerle, Lebanon, IN: Studio P/R, Inc., 1975.
[2] Sherman Oaks, CA: Roerick Music Co., 1976.

associated with a chord symbol need to be played, whether it be a scale or broken chord, but if they are, the manner in which they are presented should be less of an exercise-like undertaking.

This is the point at which patterns are very helpful. Patterns and their practice help the improviser to aurally understand groupings of notes and chords in a progression. It also helps increase technical facility. Patterns can be long or short, simple or complex, or anything in between. The student could begin easy patterning through the use of broken scales, scales in thirds, digital fragments of scales, and so on. These can also be practiced in the manner that the scales and chords were practiced.

Several good books for pattern study include *Patterns for Jazz* [3] by Jerry Coker and others, and *Techniques of Improvisation* [4] by David Baker (4 Vols.), based on George Russell's *Lydian Chromatic Concept.* [5]

Patterns can be an invaluable source to the development of a solo by a young improviser. Eventually, however, patterns should not comprise the bulk of a solo. Rather, they should supplement and fill in between the hopefully creative elements of the more advanced improviser's solo.

Once the player becomes familiar with the development of patterns and has practiced many, he or she can start using these patterns with progressions.

When starting out, it is best to use chord progressions containing chords of short duration as shorter and simpler patterns can be used more easily. Eventually of course, longer chord durations and patterns to fit those durations can be practiced. After becoming at ease with playing a pattern with a progression, mixing patterns throughout will start the player toward an understanding of melodic development.

Sources for practice on chord progressions can be drawn from sheet music, fake books, hand-written progressions, and more. Another good source is found in the appendices of Coker's *Improvising Jazz.* [6]

In applying these patterns to the chords and progressions, it is important to know which scale and chord patterns fit with a particular chord in a progression and that chord's function. Two good sources containing guide charts for this are Haerle's *Scales for Improvisation* [7] and *Jazz Improvisation* [8] by Kynaston and Ricci.

No matter how advanced a player you are, always include patterns, old and new, in your practice routine.

THE BLUES One of the most common forms of progressions found is that called the "blues." It is generally thought of as having a twelve-measure structure, though some blues are of different lengths, and has a predetermined

[3] Lebanon, IN: Studio P/R, Inc., 1970.
[4] Chicago: Downbeat Music Workshop Publications, 1968.
[5] New York: Concept, 1959.
[6] Englewood Cliffs, NJ: Prentice-Hall, Inc., 1964.
[7] Lebanon, IN: Studio P/R, Inc., 1975.
[8] Englewood Cliffs, NJ: Prentice-Hall, Inc., 1978.

progression of chords. There are very many variations of blues progressions, the simplest using three basic chords. (Fig. 7-2)

Figure 7–2

A couple of good sources for practice of blues progressions can be found in Coker's *Improvising Jazz*[9] and Jamey Aebersold's *New Approach to Jazz Improvisation*[10] series of play-along albums with instruction booklets.

In learning to improvise on the blues, the easiest and most effective device to get started with is the use of the blues scale. Patterns and melodies are easy to create and the player does not have to worry so much about the chord changes.

For example, when playing a blues tune in the key of B-flat, the B-flat blues scale can be used exclusively. Another way in which the blues scale can be used is over minor chords, maybe alternating with the Dorian minor scale.

The blues scale consists of: 1, ♭3, 4, [♯4 (♭5)], 5, ♭7, and 8. Following are the twelve blues scales: (Figs. 7-3A and 7-3B)

Figure 7–3a

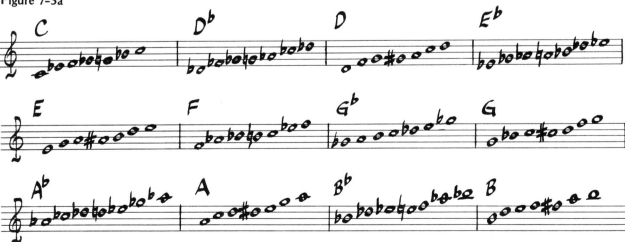

[9]Englewood Cliffs, NJ: Prentice-Hall, Inc., 1964.
[10]New Albany, IN: Jamey Aebersold. The series started in 1967, has been through various editions, and more volumes are being added to the series. There are presently 21 volumes in the series. Dates for all 21 volumes can be obtained by writing: Jamey Aebersold, 1211-D Aebersold Drive, New Albany, IN 47150

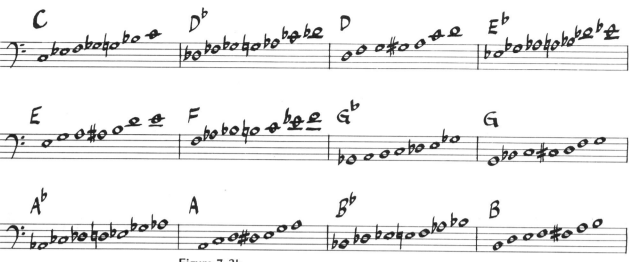

Figure 7-3b

Caution must be taken not to overuse the blues scale when improvising on blues progressions. It should be used merely as a stepping stone toward a higher level of soloing. After becoming familiar and comfortable with the blues scales, one should start experimenting with the following auxiliary blues scale for variety (transposing to all keys). (Fig. 7-4)

Figure 7-4

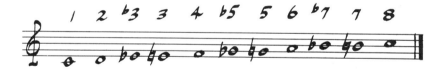

PLAYING WITH ACCOMPANIMENT

Playing with accompaniment is a very important part of learning to improvise and develop solo abilities. At this point, the student should have the needed disciplines fairly well under control and should have developed to an acceptable level the areas previously covered in this chapter. The importance of playing with accompaniment comes from the presence of interactions, the feeding off of others' ideas, the emotions involved, all the added rhythmic and harmonic aspects, and more. Naturally, mistakes will be made, but those mistakes serve as a learning device for future growth.

Many times, especially in early stages of study, it is difficult to practice with live accompaniment. Perhaps the rhythm section too is in its early stages of development and could not provide the needed quality accompaniment. Or, if they have arrived at an acceptable level of performance, the time demanded from them by other individual or group obligations may be too much to enable them to fulfill everyone's requests.

One way of circumventing these difficulties in working with live accompaniment is to work with recorded accompaniments. The Aebersold *New Approach to Jazz Improvisation* series mentioned earlier is a tremendous source of play-along accompaniment recordings. The musicians comprising the recorded rhythm section are all top-level pros who provide an excellent background. Another good source is the *Music Minus One* series of recordings covering a variety of styles.

If a good rhythm section is available, but with limited time, a tape could be made of them for practice purposes.

No matter how good or bad these sessions with accompaniment are, one should keep after it, because it is bound to aid in the growth of any player.

The development of a good "musical ear" is one of the biggest assets any musician, especially improviser, should strive for. Having proceeded through the areas of study previously mentioned in this chapter with relative success, the player should be a little freer to listen to good players and start transcribing his or her solos to gain a better understanding of solo development.

EAR TRAINING

Not only does the transcription of others' solos help improve the ear, it helps develop an inner sense and starts you on the way to "transcribing" your own musical thoughts through your instrument.

Learning to transcribe will vary in difficulty from person to person, each taking different lengths of time to develop this ability. Patience is the key, as it will pay off in the long run. Following are some suggestions to aid in learning to transcribe.

Saturate yourself with listening and reading. Start by choosing one particular artist. Obtain as many recordings of him or her as possible and read all you can about that artist. All kinds of things go into an artist's performance, including such things as lifestyle and personality. These surrounding circumstances can sometimes give perspective in understanding the artist's playing. Many jazz history books will have discographies to help in locating recordings. Two very fine references to get one started listening and reading are Jerry Coker's *Listening to Jazz*[11] and *The Jazz Idiom*.[12] Both provide many suggestions and references for further study.

Work on furthering a keen sense of pitch, intervals, progressions, tone qualities, and so on. Much of this will have taken place during the practice of scales and patterns.

Another suggestion would be using the technique of *call and response*. Practice singing back something just heard. Work on matching pitches and tone with someone else who plays your same instrument. Begin with

[11] Englewood Cliffs, NJ: Prentice-Hall, Inc., 1978.
[12] Englewood Cliffs, NJ: Prentice-Hall, Inc. 1975.

one note at a time and work up to matching a long series of notes and/or tone qualities. Swap licks. As in the preceding exercise, start short and simple, moving to longer and more complex licks.

Choose a tune to transcribe. Again, start with one that is relatively short and simple, perhaps one for which you may already know the progression or have access to a copy of the "head" (melody) and changes. Gradually work away from familiar progressions and the use of lead sheets. This will force you to develop a keener sense of listening to and hearing the progressions.

If you are using a record, it might be a good idea to put the tune on tape to save wear and tear on the record through the repeated listening you will be doing.

Listen until you are able to scat sing the solo being studied. Any call/response singing or sight-singing you do will help develop an "inner creativeness" and ability to translate musical thoughts.

Play the recording at half-speed (3 3/4 ips instead of 7 1/2 ips on a recorder, 16 rpm instead of 33 1/3 for a turntable). The result will be the passage down one octave. Do this, playing on your instrument, until you have found all the notes. In a real problematic case, set the turntable at 16 rpm for a 33 1/3 rpm record; record it at 7 1/2 ips on a tape recorder; then play it back at 3 3/4 ips. This will slow the passage down four times, sounding two octaves lower.

Next, write the solo down. Start by placing the note heads on the staff. Then, add the bar lines. Make correct notations of note durations and rhythms.

Play along with the recording (still at the slower speed), reading the notation you have written. Check for any errors, making necessary corrections.

After the notation is completely correct, return the recording to normal speed. Play along, paying special attention to the articulations, phrasings, tonal inflections, and so on of the artist and try to imitate them.

From the solo just transcribed and practiced, take favorite patterns, melodic sequences, or progressions and transpose to all keys for future practice and use.

While the most value can be derived from transcribing solos yourself, much can be gained from the study of pre-existing transcriptions. In using these, you can analyze, compare, and identify much of the contents of these solos and others. Several sources of transcriptions are *Downbeat Magazine*,[13] the *NAJE Educator Magazine*,[14] and several books for different instruments by Dave Baker entitled *Jazz Styles and Analysis*.[15]

[13]Chicago: Maher Publications. Published monthly.
[14]Manhattan, KS: The National Association of Jazz Educators. Published quarterly.
[15]Chicago: Downbeat Music Workshop Publications. *Jazz Styles and Analysis for Trombone*, rights reserved 1973. *Jazz Styles and Analysis for Alto Sax*, rights reserved 1975.

For more on ear training and development, refer to Chapter 2 of Coker's *Jazz Idiom* [16] and Chapter 5 of his *Improvising Jazz*. [17] Other good study books dealing specifically with ear training are *Interval Studies* [18] by David Mirigan, and two by Dave Baker, *A New Approach to Ear Training for Jazz Musicians* [19] and *Advanced Ear Training for Jazz Musicians*. [20]

By now, the improviser should be able to analyze and compare the different devices used in the content of a solo and start to construct his or her own solos on a more "melodic" basis. He should be able to see how scales are applied to progressions, how patterns are used, and what cliches by certain artists keep reappearing. Also, he or she should be able to recognize quotes, determine whether the solo is built from motivic development, is linear (through-composed) in nature, or is some combination thereof.

MELODIC ANALYSIS AND DEVELOPMENT

From this analysis and the practice of these devices, the improviser can apply these techniques to his or her own soloing and start to develop a unique style.

While the ability to recognize and use those components greatly aids in the development of a solo, other factors can further enhance the performance.

To a listener, a solo should present several things. One is that if a listener can predict everything that is played in a solo prior to its playing, boredom will set in. On the other hand, if listeners can predict nothing in a solo, they will probably become frustrated, quit listening, and again become bored. In order to have interest, yet maintain some mystery about it, a good solo should strive to contain about an equal mixture of predictable and unpredictable elements.

Related to keeping a solo interesting through contrast are the elements that make up the tension and release in that solo. Tension elements build excitement and energy; whereas release elements provide for a necessary relaxation after a build-up of tension.

Elements of creating tension can include things such as taking motivic development or repetition (unifying factors in form), and coupling a change of component conditions (interest-catchers in content) together in an order building in intensity. Such an order could be building up to the highest note, loudest accent, fastest motion, going from a simple to complex texture, or building to a sub-climax before rebuilding to a more climactic point.

Care must be taken not to allow tension building to go on for too long a period without interjecting some release elements. Tension can be

[16] Englewood Cliffs, NJ: Prentice-Hall, Inc., 1975.
[17] Englewood Cliffs, NJ: Prentice-Hall, Inc., 1964.
[18] Oakland, CA: Fivenote Music Publications. Contact Fivenote Music Publications, Oakland, California.
[19] Lebanon, IN: Studio P/R, Inc., 1976.
[20] Lebanon, IN: Studio P/R, Inc., 1977.

quickly released by downward motion and/or the presence of component conditions in deep contrast to the elements of tension.

Depending upon the length of solo or segment of a solo, a diagram of tension/release should look like this (Fig. 7-5):

Figure 7-5

In dealing with a solo of longer development, several of these type segments can be put together to form a solo that can be diagramed as follows (Fig. 7-6):

Figure 7-6

Each successive building of tension should be greater than the previous one, saving the "best shot" for the last. The releases should all be shorter than the building of the tensions, particularly the final release.

Some elements of contrast that are a part of tension/release are:

1. *Dynamic Contrast*   ppp–fff

2. *Rhythmic Contrast*   Flowing as opposed to syncopated, long continuous lines as opposed to lines with many spaces or rests

3. *Meter Contrast* Soloist superimposes a contrasting meter over that of the rhythm background, e.g.: three-four over four-four, five-four over four-four, seven-four over four-four, and so on

4. *Register Contrast*   Sudden shifts up or down an octave or more

5. *Pitch Contrast*   Use of scoops, bends, smears, falls, flips, and doits

6. *Timbre Contrast*   Sound alterations of normal tone production such as closing the throat, flutter-tonguing, pinching the reed, using sub-tones, growls, and fuzz-tones

No matter what instrument one plays, the ability to improvise will be greatly increased and speeded up if he or she has some basic functional abilities on the keyboard. The greatest advantage comes in the increased understanding of harmonic principles developed through the use of the keyboard. Most importantly, the student is able to hear the different harmonic traits and progressions more quickly than the student not working with the keyboard.

The keyboard provides not only an aural advantage but a visual one as well. The keyboard is arranged symmetrically throughout every octave, and a visual understanding of scales, chord constructions, intervals, and progressions can be achieved.

An excellent reference for the study of keyboard in this capacity (functional usage by nonkeyboardists) and actual specifics for study of jazz keyboard is Chapter 3 of Coker's *Jazz Idiom*.[21]

FUNCTIONAL KEYBOARD FOR ALL INSTRUMENTALISTS

The road to acquiring the ability to improvise is a long and tedious one. It will naturally vary from person to person and should be approached with a lot of patience and willingness to work hard.

CONCLUDING REMARKS ON IMPROVISATION

Remember to listen, listen, listen, and practice diligently. Investigate new recordings, new methods, and new techniques. Keep up on books, magazines, and articles. For instance, contained in the *NAJE Educator Magazine*[22] is an ongoing annotated survey of teaching materials for jazz improvisation, plus a listing of publishers and addresses. This has been an invaluable source to many educators and students alike in selecting study materials.

Keep in touch with the past, and stay aware of the present and the future.

[21] Englewood Cliffs, NJ: Prentice-Hall, Inc., 1975.
[22] Manhattan, KS: The National Association of Jazz Educators. Published quarterly.

Appendix A
The Standardization
of Stage Band Articulations*

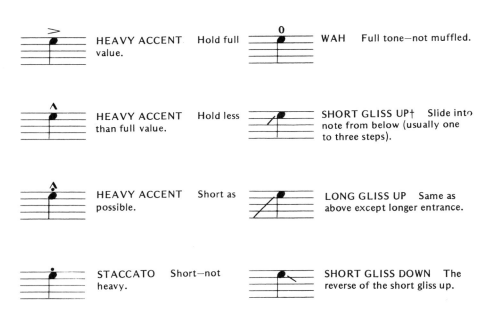

HEAVY ACCENT Hold full value.

WAH Full tone—not muffled.

HEAVY ACCENT Hold less than full value.

SHORT GLISS UP† Slide into note from below (usually one to three steps).

HEAVY ACCENT Short as possible.

LONG GLISS UP Same as above except longer entrance.

STACCATO Short—not heavy.

SHORT GLISS DOWN The reverse of the short gliss up.

*National Stage Band Camp, Inc. (Non-Profit) Stan Kenton Clinics. Used by permission.
†Note: No individual notes are heard when executing a gliss.

102

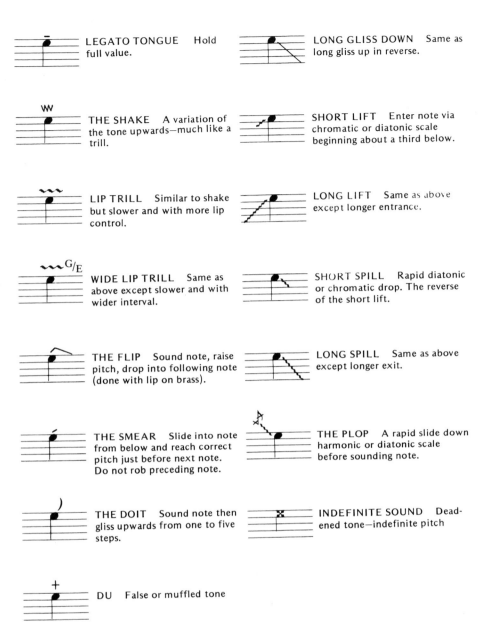

LEGATO TONGUE Hold full value.

LONG GLISS DOWN Same as long gliss up in reverse.

THE SHAKE A variation of the tone upwards—much like a trill.

SHORT LIFT Enter note via chromatic or diatonic scale beginning about a third below.

LIP TRILL Similar to shake but slower and with more lip control.

LONG LIFT Same as above except longer entrance.

WIDE LIP TRILL Same as above except slower and with wider interval.

SHORT SPILL Rapid diatonic or chromatic drop. The reverse of the short lift.

THE FLIP Sound note, raise pitch, drop into following note (done with lip on brass).

LONG SPILL Same as above except longer exit.

THE SMEAR Slide into note from below and reach correct pitch just before next note. Do not rob preceding note.

THE PLOP A rapid slide down harmonic or diatonic scale before sounding note.

THE DOIT Sound note then gliss upwards from one to five steps.

INDEFINITE SOUND Deadened tone—indefinite pitch

DU False or muffled tone

Address all inquiries to: Matt Betton, Box 724, Manhattan, Kansas 66502
National Association of Jazz Educators.

Appendix B
Jazz Chart Sources

Compiled by Ron Nethercutt, Southeastern Louisiana University, Hammond LA 70401*

Advancing Jazz Publications
186 Eldon Avenue
Columbus, OH 43204

Almo Publications
1312 N. Labrea
Hollywood, CA 90028

AJ Productions
Box 101
Beulah, MI 49617

Alnur Music
Box 343
Teaneck, NJ 07666

Alfred Music Pub. Co.
15335 Morrison Street
Sherman Oaks, CA 91403

Artistries, Inc.
64-24 Grand Ave.
Maspeth, NY 11378

William Allen Music
Box 31334
Washington, DC 20031

Art Pepper
6113 Vesper Ave.
Van Nuys, CA 90035

Note: Due to the nature of the publishing business, addresses change from time to time. Be sure to check with a local or nearby music dealer for any changes.

Assoc. Music Pub., Inc.
609 5th Ave.
New York, NY 10017

Atlantis Music
4432 Ingrahm
San Diego, CA 92109

C.L. Barnhouse Co.
Music Publishers
Oskaloosa, IA 52577

Mike Barone
Box 2156
North Hollywood, CA 91602

Eddie Barrett Orchestra
11 S. LaSalle St.
Chicago, IL 60603

Doug Beach Music
25 North 5th Ave.
Maywood, IL 60153

Berklee Press Publications
1140 Boylston Street
Boston, MA 02215

Broadcast Music, Inc.
40 West 57th St.
New York, NY 10019

California Music Library
13622 Cork St.
Garden Grove, CA 92644

Campus Music Service
Box AA
Hawthorne, CA 90250

Alf Clausen
12652 Tiara St.
North Hollywood, CA 91607

John Combes Music
Box 8025
Van Nuys, CA 91409

Contemporary Publications
562 Eastvale Drive
Ottowa, Ontario
Canada KLJ6Z3

Bill Cowling
4430 Tremont Rd.
Evansville, IN 47710

Creative Jazz Composers
Box T
Bowie, MD 20715

Creative World Music Pub.
2340 Sawtelle Blvd.
Los Angeles, CA 90064

Criteria Publications
P.O. Box 21637
San Jose, CA 95151

Dave Diggs Publishers
Box 2601-L
Anaheim, CA 92804

Chuck Dollens Music
P.O. Box 5742
Orange, CA 92667

Dorian Music Co.
2900 Ridgeway
St. Louis, MO 63114

Downbeat Music
Workshop Publications
222 W. Adams St.
Chicago, IL 60606

DVS Publications
1115 Funston Ave.
Pacific Grove, CA 93950

Edutainment Pub. Co.
P.O. Box 769
New York, NY 10019

Ellis Music Enterprises
5436 Auckland Ave.
North Hollywood, CA 91601

Emanon Music Co.
235 Gallatin St. NW
Washington, DC 20011

Ethical Music Publishers
Box 512
Hollywood, CA 90028

Etoile Music, Inc.
Pub. Division
Shell Lake, WI 54871

Federal City Publishers
c/o Rick Henderson
235 Gallatin St. NW
Washington, DC 20011

First Place Music Pub., Inc.
12754 Ventura Blvd.
Studio City, CA 91604

Fivenote Music Publications
Oakland, CA

Forefront Music
1945 Wilmette Ave.
Wilmette, IL 60091

Bill Fritz Orchestrations
1229 Geneva Street
Glendale, CA 91207

Richard Fritz Arranging Service
7373 W. 83rd Street
Los Angeles, CA 90045

Giant Steps
612 N. Sepulveda Blvd.
Los Angeles, CA 90049

Hal Leonard Publishing Co.
8112 West Bluemound Rd.
Milwaukee, WI 53213

Harris Music Publishers
Box 1356
Fort Worth, TX 76101

Neal Hefti Music, Inc.
Box 571
Encino, CA 91426

Hinshaw Music, Inc.
Box 470
Chapel Hill, NC 27514

Byron Hoyt Sheet Music
190 10th Street
San Francisco, CA 94103

Hulaws Publishing Co.
Box 5578
Inglewood, CA 90303

Jazz Education Press
Box 802
Manhatten, KS 66502

J.D. Music Publications
Box 1793
Monterey, CA 93940

Frank Jordan
1172 N. Dierra Bonita
Pasadena, CA 91104

Kaercea Music
P.O. Box 392
Roxburg, MA 02119

Kendor Music, Inc.
Music Publishers
Delevan, NY 14142

Kosmic Enterprises
Box 13366 N.T. Station
Denton, TX 76203

KSM Publications
Box 3819
Dallas, TX 75208

Tom Kubis Music Pub.
21462 Pacific Coast Hwy. Sp. 35
Huntington Beach, CA 92648

Ladd McIntosh
4444 Wallace Lane
Salt Lake City, UT 84117

Laissez-Faire Music Publishing Co.
Lake Dallas, TX 75065

Las Vegas Music Co.
Box 5812
Las Vegas, NV 89102

Lantana Music Publishers
22118 Lantana Court
Castro Valley, CA 94546

Norman Lee Publishing Co.
Box 2733
Wichita, KS 67201

David Leech
5140 Crenshaw Blvd., Apt. 102
Los Angeles, CA 90043

Life Line Music Press
Box 338
Agoura, CA 91301

Lohorn's Original Charts
4604 Woodmoore View Circle
Chattanooga, TN 37411

Maggio Music Press
Box 9717-C
North Hollywood, CA 91609

Richard Maltby Music
Box 3058
Santa Monica, CA 90403

Marina Music Service
Box 2452
San Leandro, CA 94577

Matteson-Stafford Music
10776 Village Rd., Apt. A
Dallas, TX 75203

Menza and Piestrup
12328 Magnolia Blvd.
North Hollywood, CA 91607

Midnight Sun Music Pub.
23274 Park Ensenada
Calabasas, CA 91302

Mission Music Publications
22118 Lantana Court
Castro Valley, CA 64546

M.J.Q. Music, Inc.
200 West 57th Street
New York, NY 10019

MSN Productions
2103 12th Avenue
East Seattle, WA 98102

Music Endeavors
15631 Lexington Circle
Minnetonka, MN 55343

"Music 70"
Box 706
Pittsburg, CA 94565

Musicians' Publications
Box 95
West Trenton, NJ 98628

Music Suite
1351 ¼ N. Highland
Hollywood, CA 90028

Ralph Mutchler
Dept. of Music
Olympia College
Bremerton, WA 98310

Oliver Nelson Originals
Box 90460
Worldway Postal Center
Los Angeles, CA 90009

Dick Noel Enterprises
Box 3166
Hollywood, CA 90028

Marius Nordal, Music Dept.
Highline Community College
Seattle, WA 98109

Palisades Publications
Box 35216
Los Angeles, CA 90035

P and R Music Publishers
Box 35216
Los Angeles, CA 90035

Penner Music Productions
5180 De Burn Drive
San Diego, CA 92105

Phantom Music
1514 Spruce Street
Iowa City, IA 52240

Outrageous Mother, Inc.
Box 511
Lewisville, TX 75067

Outstanding Records
Box 2111
Huntington Beach, CA 92647

Plus Music Co., Inc.
101 W. 25th Street
San Mateo, CA 94403

John Prince
2050 Volk Avenue
Long Beach, CA

Recorded Charts, LTD.
Box 171862
San Diego, CA 92117

Frank Richards
61 E. Mt. Pleasant Ave.
Livingston, NJ 17039

Dan Sanbanovich
1947 A Fell St.
San Francisco, CA 94117

Dick Shearer
P.O. Box 156
Dayton, OH 45406

Sierra Music Publications
Box 5433
Pasadena, CA 91107

Sorenson/Dolven Music Co.
41 Sutter Street
San Francisco, CA 94104

Studio 4 Productions
Box 266
Northridge, CA 91328

Studio P/R Inc.
224 S. Lebanon St.
Lebanon, IN 46052

Sunrise Artistries, Inc.
64-24 Grand Avenue
Maspeth, NY 11378

Don Sylvia
Box 77
Hampton, ME 04444

Time Revolution
1504 Melton Rd.
Lutherville, MD 21093

Fred Wayne-Arranger
501 Taylor Avenue
Glen Ellyn, IL 60137

Western International Music
3859 Holt Avenue
Los Angeles, CA 90034

Wolking Music Publications
1349 Vine Street
Salt Lake City, UT 84121

Wynn Music
Box 739
Orinda, CA 94563

Appendix C
Reference Materials

The purpose of the inclusion of this type of appendix is to provide a basis of reference for anyone wishing to further himself in the world of jazz participation.

The inclusions are by no means a complete listing of all materials, methods, and references available to the reader. They are not necessarily the best on the market nor can they meet everyone's individual needs. They are *among* those that have been found to be the most widely used.

This author would like to make special mention of membership in the *National Association of Jazz Educators* (NAJE). This, more than any one other source, has provided the most comprehensive and widespread exposure to all facets of jazz for many people through the *NAJE Educator* magazine, newsletters, annual national convention, and participation in contests, festivals, meetings, etc. For further information, write:

NAJE
Box 724
Manhattan, KS 66502

WOODWINDS   **DeFranco, B.,** *Buddy DeFranco on Jazz Improvisation* (clarinet), Famous Solos Enterprises.

Gerard, C., *Jazz Riffs for Flute, Saxophone, Trumpet, and Other Treble Instruments,* Music Sales Corp.

Lateef, Y., *Flute Book of the Blues,* Fana Music.

Laws, H., *Flute Improvisations,* Armstrong/EDU/tainment.

McGee, A., *Improvisation for Flute,* Berklee Press.

McGee, A., *Improvisation for Saxophone,* Berklee Press.

Miedema, H., *Jazz Styles and Analysis for Alto Sax,* Downbeat Music Workshop Pub.

Most, S., *Jazz Flute Conceptions,* Gwyn Pub.

Nelson, O., *Patterns for Saxophone,* Noslen Music.

Niehaus, L., *Jazz Improvisation for Saxophone,* Professional Drum Shop.

Viola, J., *The Technique of the Flute,* Berklee Press.

Viola, J., *The Technique of the Saxophone* (3 vols.), Berklee Press.

BRASS   **Baker, D.,** *Contemporary Techniques for the Trombone,* Charles Colin.

Baker, D., *Jazz Styles and Analysis for Trombone,* Downbeat Music Workshop Publications

Baron, A., *Jazz Riffs for Trombone,* Music Sales Corp.

Gerard, C., *Jazz Riffs for Flute, Saxophone, Trumpet, and Other Treble Instruments,* Music Sales Corp.

James, H., *Studies and Improvisations* (trumpet), Big 3.

Kotwica, R., and J. Viola, *Chord Studies for Trumpet,* Berklee Press.

McNeil, J., *Jazz Trumpet Techniques,* Studio P/R.

Slone, K. (trans.), and J. Aebersold (ed.), *28 Modern Jazz Trumpet Solos,* Studio P/R.

Terry, C., and P. Rizzo, *Let's Talk Trumpet,* Creative Jazz Composers.

Wilson, P., and J. Viola, *Chord Studies for Trombone,* Berklee Press.

RHYTHM   **Appice, C.,** *Realistic Hi Hats* (drums), Warner Bros.

Appice, C., *Realistic Rock* (drums), Big 3.

Bay, M., *Rhythm Guitar Chord System,* Mel Bay Publ.

Berkowitz, S., *Improvisation Through Keyboard Harmony,* Prentice-Hall, Inc.

Brown, R., *Bass Method,* First Place Music, Publ.

Burns, R., and S. Feldstein, *Drum Set Artistry,* Alfred Music Co.

Carter R., *Building A Jazz Bass Line* (2 vols.), Ronald Carter Music Co.

Carter, R., *Comprehensive Bass Method,* Chas. Hansen.

Chapin, J., *Advanced Technique for the Modern Drummer* (2 vols.), Jim Chapin.

Cohen, M., *Understanding Latin Rhythms* (2 vols.), Latin Percussion.

Coryell, L., *Improvisation from Rock To Jazz* (guitar-LP and booklet), Guitar Player Records.

Dawson, A., and D. DeMicheal, *A Manual for the Modern Drummer,* Berklee Press.

Delp, R., and J. Viola, *Chord Studies for Mallet Instruments,* Berklee Press.

Delp, R., *Multi-Pitch Rhythm Studies for Drums,* Berklee Press.

Delp, R., *Vibraphone Technique,* Berklee Press.

Fink, R., *Drum Set Reading,* Alfred Music Co.

Friedman, D., *Vibraphone Technique: Dampening and Pedaling,* Berklee Press.

Garson, L., and J. Stewart (ed.), *Wes Montgomery Jazz Guitar Method,* Big 3.

Gray, J., *Bluesblues* (piano), Mitchell Madison.

Green, I., *Show Drumming,* J.R. Publ.

Haerle, D., *Jazz Improvisation for Keyboard Players* (3 vols.), Studio P/R.

Haerle, D., *Jazz/Rock Voicings for the Contemporary Keyboard Player,* Studio P/R.

Hammick, V., *Electric Bass Technique* (2 vols.), Salena Pub.

Kaye, C., *Contemporary Bass Lines,* Warner Bros.

Kaye, C., *Electric Bass Lines,* Gwyn Pub.

Kessel, B., *The Guitar,* Studio P/R.

Konowitz, B., *The Complete Rock Piano Method,* Alfred Music.

LaPorta, J., *Functional Piano for the Improvisor,* Kendor Music, Inc.

Leavitt, W., *Melodic Rhythms for Guitar,* Berklee Press.

Leavitt, W., *A Modern Method for Guitar* (3 vols.), Berklee Press.

Lee, R., *Jazz Guitar* (2 vols.), Chas. Hansen.

Mehegan, J., *Contemporary Styles for the Jazz Pianist,* Carl Fischer.

Mehegan, J., *Famous Jazz Style Piano Folio,* Chas. Hansen.

Mehegan, J., *Jazz Improvisation* (4 vols.), Hyperion Press.

Mehegan, J., *The Jazz Pianist* (3 vols.), Carl Fischer.

Mehegan, J., *Studies in Jazz Harmony*, Carl Fisher.

Mehegan, J., *Styles for the Jazz Pianist* (3 vols.), Carl Fischer.

Mintz, B., *Different Drummers*, Music Sales Corp.

Montgomery, M., and D. Baker (ed.), *The Monk Montgomery Electric Bass Method*, Studio P/R.

Pass, J., *Joe Pass Guitar Chords*, Warner Bros.

Pass, J., *The Joe Pass Guitar Method*, Theodore Presser Co.

Pass, J., and B. Thrasher, *Joe Pass Guitar Style*, Gwin Pub.

Pickering, J., *The Drummer's Cookbook*, Mel Bay Publ.

Progris, J., *A Modern Method for Keyboard Study* (4 vols. and suppl.), Berklee Press.

Rector, J., *Guitar Chord Progressions*, Mel Bay Publ.

Reid, R., *The Evolving Bassist*, Myriad Limited.

Reid, R., *Evolving Upward Bass Book II*, Myriad Limited.

Rizzo, P., *Spread Chord Voicings* (piano), Palisades Pub.

Rothman, J., *Independent Thinking*, J.R. Publ.

Rothman, J., *Jazz Around the Drums*, J.R. Publ.

Rothman, J., *Jazz Bible of Coordination*, J.R. Publ.

Rothman, J., *Recipes with Paradiddles Around the Drums*, J.R. Publ.

Sandole, A., *Jazz Piano Left Hand*, Adolph Sandole.

Smith, J., *The Johnny Smith Approach to Guitar* (2 vols.), Mel Bay Publ.

Swain, A., *Four-Way Keyboard System* (3 vols.), Creative Music.

Wheaton, J., *Basic Modal Improvisation Techniques for Keyboard Instruments*, First Place Music Publ.

GENERAL/ALL INSTRUMENTS

Aebersold, J., *A New Approach to Jazz Improvisation* (series of LP's and booklets), J.A. Publ.

Baker, D., *Advanced Ear Training for Jazz Musicians*, Studio P/R.

Baker, D., *Advanced Improvisation*, Downbeat Music Workshop Publ.

Baker, D., *A New Approach to Ear Training for Jazz Musicians*, Studio P/R.

Baker, D., *Jazz Improvisation*, Downbeat Music Workshop Publications

Baker, D., *Jazz Improvisation Method: Strings* (Book I: violin and viola, Book II: cello and bass), Mahler Publ.

Baker, D., *Jazz Pedagogy (A Comprehensive Method of Jazz Education for Teacher and Student)*, Downbeat Music Workshop Publications

Baker, D., *Techniques of Improvisation* (4 vols.), Downbeat Music Workshop Publications.

Betton, M., and C. Peters, *"Take One" Improvisation,* Neil A. Kjos.

Bishop, W., *A Study in Fourths,* Caldon Publ.

Bower, B., *Complete Chords and Progressions,* Chas. Colin.

Brandt, C., and C. Roemer, *Standardized Chord Symbol Notation,* Roerick Music Co.

Brown, R., and S. Brown, *An Introduction to Jazz Improvisation* (LP and book), Creative World.

Carubia, M., *The Sound of Improvisation* (book and cassette), Alfred Music.

Coker, J., *Improvising Jazz,* Prentice-Hall, Inc.

Coker, J., *The Jazz Idiom,* Prentice-Hall, Inc.

Coker, J., *Listening to Jazz,* Prentice-Hall, Inc.

Coker, J. et al., *Patterns for Jazz,* Studio P/R.

Colin, C. and D. Schaeffer, *The Encyclopedia of Scales,* Chas. Colin.

Collver, R., *Improvisng Jazz Etudes,* B.C. Music Publ.

Collver, R., *100 Jazz Cliches,* B.C. Music Publ.

Curtis, W., *First Steps to Ear Training,* Berklee Press.

Deutsch, M., *Lexicon of Symmetric Scales and Tonal Patterns,* Chas. Colin.

Gambino, T., *Jazz Patterns for the Instrumentalist,* Sunrise Artistries, Inc.

Gridley, M., *Jazz Styles,* Prentice-Hall, Inc.

Grove, D., *Applied Modal Improvisation,* Vol. IV, Dick Grove Publ.

Grove, D., *The Encyclopedia of Basic Harmony and Theory Applied to Improvisation on All Instruments* (3 vols.), Dick Grove Publ.

Grove, D., *Fundamentals of Modern Harmony,* Dick Grove Publ.

Haerle, D., *Scales for Jazz Improvisation,* Studio P/R.

Hall, M.E., *Modern Stage Band Techniques,* Southern Music Co.

Kynaston, T., and R. Ricci, *Jazz Improvisation,* Prentice-Hall, Inc.

LaPorta, J., *A Guide to Improvisation,* Berklee Press.

LaPorta, J., *Ear Training Phase I,* Berklee Press.

La Porta, J., *Developing the Stage Band,* Berklee Press.

LaPorta, J., *Tonal Organization of Improvisational Techniques,* Kendor Music, Inc.

Minasi, D., *Musicians' Manual for Chord Substitution,* Sunrise Artistries, Inc.

Mirigian, D., *For Players Only: Jazz Resources,* Fivenote Music Publ.

Mirigian, D., *Interval Studies,* Fivenote Music Publ.

Mirigian, D., *Pentatonic Patterns,* Fivenote Music Publ.

Ricker, R., *New Concepts in Linear Improvisation,* Studio P/R.

Ricker, R., *Pentatonic Scales for Jazz Improvisation,* Studio P/R.

Ricker, R., *Technique Development in Fourths for Jazz Improvisation,* Studio P/R.

Rizzo, P., *Creative Melodic Technique Used in Jazz Improvisation,* Modern Music School.

Rizzo, P., *Ear Training Based on 12 Tones,* Palisades Publ.

Rizzo, P., *First Step to Improvisation,* Palisades Publ.

Russell, G., *The Lydian Chromatic Concept of Tonal Organization for Improvisation,* Concept Pub. Co.

Schilhinger, J., *Kaleidophone,* Chas. Colin.

Sebesky, G., *The Elementary Stage Band Book,* Studio P/R.

Sherman, H., *Techniques and Materials for Stage Band,* Creative World.

Slonimsky, N., *Thesaurus of Scales and Melodic Patterns,* Chas. Scribner and Sons.

Terry, C., and P. Rizzo, *The Interpretation of the Jazz Language,* M.A.S. Pub. Co.

Wiskirchen, G., *Developmental Techniques for the Jazz Ensemble Musician,* Berklee Press.

MAGAZINES

Billboard
P.O. Box 2156
Radnor, PA 19089

CODA
P.O. Box 87 Station J
Toronto, Ontario
M4J4X8 Canada

Crescendo
P.O. Box 187
Williston Park, NY 11596

Downbeat
222 W. Adams St.
Chicago, IL 60606

Guitar Player
P.O. Box 615
12333 Saratoga-Sunnyville Rd.
Saratoga, CA 95070

The Instrumentalist
1418 Lake St.
Evanston, IL 60204

The Music Educators Journal
8150 Leesburg Pike—Suite 601
Vienna, VA 22180

Music Handbook (Downbeat)
222 W. Adams St.
Chicago, IL 60606

Music Journal
370 Lexington Ave.
New York, NY 10017

NAJE Educator
P.O. Box 724
Manhattan, KS 66502

PTM World of Music
434 S. Wabash Ave.
Chicago, IL 60605

Radio Free Jazz! U.S.A.
3212 Pennsylvania Ave., SE.
Washington, D.C. 20020

Rolling Stone
P.O. Box 2983
Boulder, CO 80302

The School Musician
4 E. Clinton
Joliet, IL 60431

Bibliography

Aebersold, Jamey, *A New Approach to Jazz Improvisation* (multi-volume), New Albany, IN: Jamey Aebersold, various dates.

Apel, Willi, *Harvard Dictionary of Music* (2nd ed.), Cambridge, MA: The Belknap Press of the Harvard University Press, 1969.

Baker, David N., *Jazz Pedagogy (A Comprehensive Method of Jazz Education for Teacher and Student),* Chicago, IL: Downbeat Music Workshop Publications, 1979.

Betton, Matt, Sr., (ed.), *NAJE Educator,* Manhattan, KS: The National Association of Jazz Educators, various issues.

Bessom, Malcolm E., *Supervising the Successful School Music Program,* West Nyack, NY: Parker Publishing Company, Inc., 1969.

Bessom, Malcolm E., Alphonse M. Tatarunis, and Samuel L. Forcucci, *Teaching Music in Today's Secondary Schools,* New York: Holt, Rinehart and Winston, Inc., 1974.

Brandt, Carl, and Clinton Roemer, *Standardized Chord Symbol Notation* (2nd ed.), Sherman Oaks, CA: Roerick Music Co., 1976.

Carman, Charles (ed.), *Down Beat,* Chicago, IL: Maher Publications, various issues.

Coker, Jerry, *Improvising Jazz,* Englewood Cliffs, NJ: Prentice-Hall, Inc., 1964.

Coker, Jerry, *The Jazz Idiom,* Englewood Cliffs, NJ: Prentice-Hall, Inc., 1975.

Coker, Jerry, *Listening to Jazz,* Englewood Cliffs, NJ: Prentice-Hall, Inc., 1978.

Coker, Jerry et al., *Patterns for Jazz,* Lebanon, IN: Studio P/R, Inc., 1970.

Dexter, Dave, Jr., *The Jazz Story,* Englewood Cliffs, NJ: Prentice-Hall, Inc., 1964.

Ferguson, Tom, and Sandy Feldstein, *The Jazz Rock Ensemble,* Port Washington, NY: Alfred Publishing Co., Inc., 1976.

Good, Carter V., (ed.), *Dictionary of Education,* New York: McGraw-Hill Book Company, 1973.

Gridley, Mark C., *Jazz Styles,* Englewood Cliffs, NJ: Prentice-Hall, Inc., 1978.

Haerle, Dan, *Jazz/Rock Voicings for the Contemporary Keyboard Player,* Lebanon, IN: Studio P/R, Inc., 1974.

Haerle, Dan, *Scales for Improvisation,* Lebanon, IN: Studio P/R, Inc., 1975.

Hall, Dr. M.E., *Modern Stage Band Techniques,* San Antonio, TX: Southern Music Company, 1975.

Kennan, Kent Wheeler, *The Technique of Orchestration* (2nd ed.), Englewood Cliffs, NJ: Prentice-Hall, Inc., 1970.

Kynaston, Trent P., and Robert J. Ricci, *Jazz Improvisation,* Englewood Cliffs, NJ: Prentice-Hall, Inc., 1978.

Leonhard, Charles, and Robert W. House, *Foundations and Principles of Music Education* (2nd ed.), New York: McGraw-Hill Book Company, 1972.

Maher, Jack, (ed.), *Downbeat Music Handbook* (various issues), Chicago, IL: Maher Publications, various dates.

Prescott, Gerald R., and Lawrence W. Chidester, *Getting Results With School Bands,* Minneapolis, MN: Paul A. Schmitt Music Co., 1938.

Sherman, Hal, *Techniques and Materials for Stage Band,* Los Angeles, CA: Creative World Music Publications, 1976.

Wiskirchen, Rev. George C.S.C., *Developmental Techniques for the Jazz Ensemble Musician,* Boston, MA: Berklee Press Publications, 1961.